FIRST TIME DAD

PREGNANCY HANDBOOK FOR DADS-TO-BE

STEVEN BELL

ISBN: 978-1-951791-41-4

Visit:

avaburke.org/dad

Table of Contents

Introduction

If you are reading this, you might either have recently found out that the woman in your life is pregnant, you are "pulling the goalie," and you're going to start trying to get pregnant, or that you are just curious about what you should expect from fatherhood. My wife and I were extremely fortunate to conceive within our first few attempts, so it was a little more surprising for us to discover this news than it might be for some couples who have been struggling to conceive for years. Regardless of whether you conceived via the old-fashioned way, intrauterine insemination, in vitro fertilization, or any other way, I feel that I have some insight to offer to other dads as they begin their journey to fatherhood. I must be honest: at the time of writing this content, my son is just over three months old, so I am still in my relative infancy (pun intended) of fatherhood. However, I still feel that sharing my experiences can be helpful to other guys as they prepare for the nine months of pregnancy and the first few months following delivery, which is sometimes referred to as the fourth trimester. Luckily for me, my wife is a pediatrician, so she was able to give me more of a heads up than some other dudes out there, which was tremendously helpful. As a result, I feel it is my duty to paraphrase the guidance she gave me and sprinkle in my own anecdotes to help fellow dads adapt to this life-changing event. Even though I have not been a father for long, I can say with absolute certainty that it has truly been the most special experience of my life so far, and I cannot express how much joy your little one can bring you. Be excited, be afraid, be prepared, and be surprised. It is a rollercoaster of emotions, but you will come out as a stronger person.

Part I:
We Did It!

Congratulations, sniper – the orgasm counted this time! Your sperm has successfully infiltrated your woman's egg, and the cells are beginning to multiply. Before we get into what to expect in the nine months of pregnancy and the first few months of fatherhood – which I will cover in Part II and Part III, respectively – I would like to give you a more detailed overview of things to keep in mind as you and your lady progress through this tumultuous time. It is important for both of you to remain calm, confirm the pregnancy with a healthcare provider, and exercise cautionary optimism over the next few months – and particularly over the first 12 weeks of pregnancy. Give your lady a high five, make your battle plans, and man your stations.

Chapter 1:
Positive Pregnancy Test – What Now?

First of all, take a deep breath. Remain calm. Whether you intended to conceive or not, the best thing you can do is try to relax for your sake as well as for your lady's sake. When I first heard that my wife was pregnant, I was almost in disbelief. Part of that was because we had only bumped uglies during her optimal time of the month a few times since pulling the goalie, and part of it was due to me being away from home for a couple of months on a work assignment in Chicago. I assure you, she remained faithful, which was confirmed by my son's uncanny resemblance to me. I fully expected that we would have to try several times – like most people – before we could conceive, but I guess we are some of the lucky ones. At-home pregnancy tests are only effective following a missed period, and the time between ovulation and a woman's period is approximately two-to-three weeks, so by the time the positive pregnancy test occurs, your lady is already several weeks pregnant. I had only been away from her for about a month when we discovered the news, and needless to say, my mind was racing a mile per minute.

As I mentioned, my wife is a pediatrician, but she was still completing her residency when we started trying, and on the other hand, I was completing my graduate degree in addition to working. For those unfamiliar with the lifestyle of a resident physician, they work extremely long and odd hours and are exposed to many sick patients. All of this is to say that it may not have been the *best* time for us to try and conceive, but at this point, it did not really matter. Ready or not, my world was about to change, and so is yours if you are reading this.

It is critical to remain pragmatic when faced with the challenges that life throws at you, and do your best not to succumb to your innate emotional response and crumble under what feels like immense pressure. You and your lady are a team, and right now, she needs you to be a source of calm. My wife was out with friends earlier that night, and the thought had come to her that she had not had her normal period and that she might as well pee on the stick just in case. I was at a Chicago Cubs game at Wrigley Field when I got the text that said, "we need to talk." Those four words generally instill fear in most people, and the experience was no different for me. I made an excuse to leave the game in the seventh inning, caught the "L" at Addison Station, and made my way to my temporary residence before we could speak in privacy on the phone. She made me do the "guess what" game, which I am really not a fan of, but I figured something was up and correctly guessed that we now had a bun in the oven.

As I said, I almost could not believe what had happened. I asked her on the number of pregnancy tests she had taken – as false positives are certainly not *unheard of* – but she had taken three, and all three had a very solid line indicating that she was, in fact, pregnant. She sounded exasperated on the phone as she was also in disbelief. I could also sense panic in her voice, but I did my best to remain calm even though I was freaking out internally. I reassured my wife that everything was going to be fine. We obviously needed to get

8

confirmation that this pregnancy was real and not some crazy coincidence of three false positives (which, let's face it, is nearly impossible). I think part of me was actually hoping that she wasn't pregnant, as she was coming to visit me in Chicago in a couple of weeks. I was actually looking forward to taking her to some of the cocktail bars, breweries, and nightclubs that I found to be fun. Obviously, a pregnant woman can still be a patron at these establishments without imbibing, but that is really the point of going to them. Regardless, we talked for about an hour that night and made plans for the morning to seek confirmation.

Despite the nervousness we both were experiencing, my staying calm — at least on the surface — seemed to ease her as we talked through the next steps. It is important for you to remember to do the same. Everything is not on fire. You can do this. Take some deep breaths. You have three quarters of a year to prepare. You and your lady are a team, and sometimes team members need to take on specific roles to achieve the desired outcome. Your role at this point in the game, just as Dr. Saperstein told Ben in Parks and Rec, when they found out that Leslie was pregnant with triplets, is to be Matthew McConaughey in a hammock on the beach. Panic and fear, although completely understandable reactions are not helpful to your team. Remain calm. Alright, alright, alright?

Getting confirmation with a healthcare provider is the logical next step. Your lady can pee on as many sticks as she wants, but for me, things got real once we had our first ultrasound. I could see the little flicker and hear the fast-paced heartbeat. However, there are some tests that can and should be done before scheduling the ultrasound. As soon as there is any question as to whether your lady is pregnant, schedule a visit with a healthcare provider to have her blood tested. There are two types of blood tests to check for pregnancy: one is a qualitative blood test, which checks to see if the hormone hCG (Human Chorionic Gonadotropin), which is the "pregnancy hormone," is actually present in her blood; and a quantitative blood test, which measures the exact amount of hCG in her blood. These are the first official tests to check for pregnancy, and then the ultrasound will typically follow.

In case you were curious, the at-home pee-on-the-stick pregnancy tests also check for the presence of hCG, so the blood tests are similar in that regard. However, scheduling this visit with a healthcare provider gives your lady the opportunity to confirm the pregnancy in a controlled setting as well as make a plan and schedule for recurring prenatal visits throughout the pregnancy. There are some sources out there that say the blood test is not absolutely necessary, and they are right – it is not essential to have that step done as your lady's OBGYN can also confirm it with a transvaginal ultrasound. However, the blood test can provide the information they need to confirm the pregnancy. The blood test consists of at least two blood draws, which occur approximately 48 hours apart. As mentioned, there are qualitative and quantitative aspects of the blood test. The hCG levels in your lady's blood should double about every 48 hours, so these two blood draws will enable the healthcare provider to determine if a miscarriage or ectopic pregnancy occurred, or if the pregnancy is progressing as it should in the early stages.

Typically, the heartbeat of the fetus is visible via ultrasound around the 8-week mark, although sometimes it may take longer than that to see or hear the heartbeat. If the results of the blood test confirmed the pregnancy, but the ultrasound was inconclusive, do not panic. Everything could very well still be fine, and panicking or worrying about it does not do you or your lady any good. Throughout my wife's pregnancy, she had a few ultrasounds performed, and it seemed that the sonographer (i.e., the person performing the ultrasound) was either still training or had recently completed their training and struggled to find the heartbeat. When this happened, we had a few minutes of frozen panic as we assumed the worst – that my wife had miscarried. It is estimated that miscarriage happens in about one in four recognized pregnancies, with the lion's share (around 85%) occurring in the first trimester. This was my wife's first pregnancy (at least her first known pregnancy), and it seems that miscarriage rates are higher in the first pregnancy. It is certainly easier said than done, but you have to try your possible best to remain calm if the ultrasound appears to be inconclusive. When the sonographer did struggle to find the fetus in utero, the healthcare provider came in and found the heartbeat within seconds, which eased the tension and made us relax. The first time I heard the heartbeat of our unborn child (whose sex was still undetermined at that time), it made me feel emotional. I am not someone who is brought close to tears at something like this. I was not even remotely brought to tears when I heard the ultrasound recordings of my unborn nieces and nephews when my siblings and their significant others were expecting – but this was my child. It is truly a remarkable feeling the first time you hear the quick heartbeat and see the tiny flicker, which is the fetus on the ultrasound, and you think: we did that. We made [the beginnings of] a human being.

What made these initial visits worse for me was that I was out of the state and "attended" these visits via FaceTime with my wife. I really wished that I could have been there in person in the first few visits to enable me comfort my wife with physical touch – especially when the sonographer struggled to find the heartbeat. So, guys, if you can, please make a point to attend all of such visits with your lady, as I know that my wife also wished I was there in person. I know that I will certainly do everything I can to be there in person for all early visits in subsequent pregnancies, but I really hope that occurs only one to two more times at an absolute maximum. I have three siblings myself, and we are all within seven years of each other. I think my wife and I are comfortable with having two to three kids, but more power to my parents for getting it done with four (and for other parents out there who have more than that). At any rate, getting confirmation with a healthcare provider is a crucial initial step for you and your lady to begin making all necessary plans throughout the pregnancy and prepare for bringing your little one home after delivery. However, be prepared to temper expectations.

After your healthcare provider confirms that you have successfully knocked up your lady, you may want to spread the good news to all family and friends – especially if you two have been trying for a while to make this happen. However, be careful. I mentioned earlier that many first pregnancies – and a fair amount of pregnancies in general – end in miscarriage in the first trimester. Imagine that your wife is eight weeks pregnant, and you just got the confirmation from your healthcare provider, and you post the good news all over social media and text all your family and friends, only for her to have a miscarriage in the next two or three weeks. It will be devastating. You will not be able to spread this news as cheerfully as before, so it would inevitably lead to other people asking you or your wife – how things are going with the pregnancy, when they are, in fact, not going well at all. It can cause a significant amount of emotional damage. Believe me – I wanted to share our good news with everyone, but my wife responsibly held me back from doing so. I am glad she did, as I later found out that one of her good friends had just found out that she had a miscarriage around the same time. My recommendation to all guys is: be excited but keep things quiet. Practice cautious optimism.

My wife confirmed her pregnancy with our healthcare provider around June 25th, and at the time of this visit, she was approximately eight weeks pregnant. We wanted to share it with our parents and siblings (and their significant others), but we did not want to expand the circle of those who were "in the know" beyond that. My parents came to visit me in Chicago for a weekend, and I called my wife over FaceTime as I walked into their hotel. I was giddy with excitement and could not wait to tell them the good news. They were completely unsuspecting, thinking that I was just on FaceTime with my wife in their presence so that they could also say hello to her as they had not seen each other for several months at that point (we live several states apart). Now we played the "guess what" game with my parents, but they were unable to render a guess before my wife blurted out, "I'm pregnant!" Needless to say, my parents were extremely excited. At the time, my older brother had two young boys, my older sister had a son and two daughters, and my younger sister was several months pregnant with twins. This would make our baby my parents' eighth grandchild.

My mom jokes that she put in an order for 12 grandchildren, so her children were about two-thirds of the way there. My older brother and older sister said they are absolutely done having kids, so I guess this puts the onus on my younger sister and me to reach that goal. It is possible, but my younger sister will need to take one for the team if that goal is to be achieved, as my wife and I are going to keep our numbers down to two or three children. At any rate, I digress… my parents were ecstatic, and we went out for drinks to celebrate (but no alcohol allowed back at home for my wife!). We told her parents the good news as well, and this would make grandbaby number two for them, about which they were very excited. Next, we told our siblings and their spouses over a group text, but we were very clear that we did not want the news extended beyond that group. Of course, everyone understood that. Looking back, I am happy that only our family members knew as we were receiving the love and support we wanted while also keeping our news a relative secret as Murphy's Law was always on our minds.

No more than two weeks after telling our families about the good news, we had an incident. As my wife was at work, she began bleeding from her lady bits and had to excuse herself to the bathroom for a while. What started as a little bit of blood progressed to a substantial amount of blood, and naturally, she assumed the worst had happened, and she had miscarried. Again, this would be devastating to us – especially after all of the excitement of sharing the news with our family – but it would not have been completely unfathomable. My wife bled so much that she began to get lightheaded and called me while I was at work to tell me what was going on. She was absolutely panicking on the phone, and I grew quite anxious when she explained the situation. I will never forget her saying, "I definitely miscarried," with the sense of dread and defeat in her voice. It was almost as if she felt she let me down, which is the last thing I would want on her mind while this was happening. I was very concerned for her and her safety, considering the amount of blood she told me she was losing. Thankfully, she is a resident physician and was working on rotation at a university hospital at the time, so medical help was not far away if she needed it. However, the bleeding slowed over time and stopped altogether within about 20 minutes. She was able to explain the situation to her attending physician, who let her leave her shift early to schedule a visit with our OBGYN.

My wife and I let our parents know what was going on and how it was almost certain that she had miscarried. They quickly spread this news to our siblings, who were nothing but supportive and compassionate with our situation. As a matter of fact, my brother and his wife were required to terminate their first pregnancy in the second trimester because they had a fetal anomaly that was incompatible with life, and carrying the pregnancy to the end could also have put the health of my sister-in-law at risk. I will not go into their story here, but needless to say, they were very familiar with how devastating and exhausting this rollercoaster of emotions can be. My wife and I were high with excitement after telling our family the good news, and now we felt we were back to square one. Although this would have been a difficult situation to get through, we reminded each other of how good we have it (student loans and all) compared to others who are less fortunate. However, all of our panic and worry was for nothing. My wife had an ultrasound a day or two after this incident, and everything with the fetus appeared to be fine. She is obviously more knowledgeable about the science and medicine associated with pregnancy than I am, but to this day, she (and even her OBGYN) has no idea what happened and why she bled as much as she did. It was a scary moment followed by a sad couple of days, but our excitement returned as our OBGYN informed us there was nothing to worry about; the fetus was progressing as expected.

I share this story to reiterate the need for you to practice cautious optimism. When you first discover that your lady is pregnant, it is so difficult not to share the news with everyone. By all means, be excited – you should be! However, sequester that impulse to blurt out the news. There are so many things that can go wrong even if you and her have done everything right in the first few weeks. As Captain Picard of Star Trek said, "It is possible to commit no errors and still lose. That is not a weakness; that is life." Even if the worst does happen and she does miscarry, do not let it get you down. My wife and I have several friends who have had miscarriages in their first pregnancy, which we found out about years later, and they told us that the experience, although traumatic, brought them closer together as a couple. Keep the news of your early pregnancy to a small circle of those closest to you. Most recommendations I found relating to sharing the news with a broader audience says that it is best to wait until you are into the second trimester (i.e., after the 12-week mark) as the risk of miscarriage decreases at that point. Although it is still possible, it is less likely to occur spontaneously as it can in the first trimester. Some of you may want to keep the news confined to a smaller group for even longer, and that is fine, too. However, it will be hard to keep it as a secret once your lady's stomach starts protruding.. Although I suppose, you could just blame it on her affinity to fried foods and cake (just kidding – do NOT call your pregnant lady fat!).

Chapter 2:
Preparing for Parenthood

It is difficult to fully prepare for parenthood. You may have read several guides, set detailed plans, and feel that you are ready for the addition of a small family member (or members), but my wife and I have found out that there are new things we learn every day that no pamphlet or book will prepare you for. And, again, my wife is a pediatrician; she feels that being a mom has given her more insight into what works and what does not than the countless well-child visits she has conducted with children from all familial backgrounds over the years. With all this being said, there are still several things that are universally important in your battle preparations. These include clarifying expectations of both mom and dad, getting your finances in order as best as you can, making plans for logistics and supplies, and choosing a name for your child. As always, you and your lady are a team, and it is essential for you to involve yourself in this process so that you will be ready to hit the ground running once the little one arrives.

After your healthcare provider has confirmed the pregnancy, and things seem to be progressing as expected, as well as the due date being determined, it is important to have recurring conversations with your lady to talk about how you envision your lives after the new one is here. Ideally, you both will get some time away from work (i.e., paternity and maternity leave) so that you can limit other distractions and slowly adapt to your new lifestyle. Though, setting expectations before reaching this point can make the process smoother. One thing is certain: your old way of life is gone. Ready or not, things are about to change drastically for you. When it was just you and the lady, I guess it was so easy to be spontaneous and decide to go out to a restaurant for dinner, to a bar or a club for drinks and dancing, or to a theater to catch a late-night horror movie. I will be honest: I miss the ability to do whatever I wanted at the drop of a hat, but this is my new reality, and it is absolutely worth it. You and your lady need to discuss what both of you will expect of yourselves once your newborn is home. Are you going to be present as much as possible? You should be. Are you going to be changing diapers? Definitely. Are you going to get up in the middle of the night to feed and comfort the little one if they are fussing? You should expect to (although breastfeeding does muddy the waters here, I will discuss more on that in Part III). After all, you have 50% of the responsibility of conceiving the child in the first place, so you should have 50% of the responsibility in caring and raising your child. This is the 21st Century – women are not viewed as the only ones responsible for childcare anymore, nor should you expect your lady to carry more of the responsibility. As a matter of fact, fathers are now the primary caregiver for approximately one out of every four preschool-age children, according to the U.S. Census Bureau[1], and that should not be expected to decrease any time soon.

My wife and I spoke often about what we expected of each other as parents as we reached the second trimester, even if it was as simple as how we envisioned our daily routine would change. You need to talk to your partner and clarify what you expect from them as well as understand what they expect of you. You should also give

---

[1]   https://www.parents.com/parenting/dads/issues-trends/the-responsibilities-and-expectations-of-the-new-american-dad/

some thought as to what you expect from yourself as this can allow you to be proactive in identifying sacrifices that you will need to make in order to be prepared for the changes ahead. Clarifying these expectations between you and your partner must happen before you can hold each other accountable, and it really provides for the foundation of a healthy relationship amid the challenge on which you are about to undertake. Remember the adage *happy wife, happy life* as I have found that to be true, especially since we brought our little one home.

Unfortunately for my wife – and also for me – being a resident physician means that her maternity leave was extraordinarily short compared to more traditional maternity leave; she was only given six weeks off after delivery. She had to work many nights and 12-hour shifts (often with no days off for two weeks) following her return to work. I was in my final semester of graduate school at the time, so we had to discuss how much more responsibility I would need to take on as it related to taking care of our child. We had found a suitable daycare within a reasonable distance from our place, and I was prepared to drive our son to and from that facility before and after class while my wife was at work. I welcomed this new responsibility – even though it was out of the way, and I was primarily the only one making that trip – because my wife and I had clarified this expectation beforehand. When the time came, however, the coronavirus pandemic was just picking up, and all of my classes were moved to an online format, which enabled me to attend class without having to drive to the daycare (and potentially expose myself and my son). I suppose that is one small positive thing that came out of this pandemic from a personal perspective, but the point still stands.

I also enjoy exercising daily; it is very therapeutic for me, and it allows me to decompress. Given my wife's fluctuating schedule in addition to having a newborn, I cannot always exercise when and how I wanted. Before we brought our child home, I could go on a run outside, go to the gym, or do an at-home workout (e.g., Insanity with Shaun T!) whenever it worked best for me. When my wife is home – which is not all that often after she has returned to work – she needs to catch up on sleep while I take care of our son. The fact that I would have to compromise to limit the spontaneity of my daily workout was made quite clear in advance, and I had to adapt to a new lifestyle. This is a relatively minor example of clarifying expectations, but it highlights the point of understanding how your daily life is going to change and that the care of your newborn takes the utmost priority.

Everyone knows that it is expensive to raise a child. According to the US Department of Agriculture data, parents who have a child today will spend, on average, nearly $285,000 by the time the baby turns 18.[2] This cost is spread out over a long period, but it is nothing to sneeze at. You and your lady need to get your finances in order as best as you can prior to the arrival of your bundle of expenses – err, I mean, bundle of joy. This means that you'll be putting off on that trip to Europe any time soon and not buying the new gaming console that you have always had your eye on for some time. Generally, it means limiting any discretionary expenses, including going out to eat at restaurants or grabbing some beers or cocktails from the local watering hole. Some guys will be much better off financially than others in this regard, but speaking from the perspective of new parents who do not have much money in the bank, and who have taken on a copious amount of student loan debt (my wife dominated this with medical school debt, but I am not too far behind) – we had to make some tangible changes to our lives to

---

[2]   https://www.investopedia.com/articles/personal-finance/090415/cost-raising-child-america.asp

make these first few months work. I suggest that you look for low-cost alternatives to some of your daily routines, whether it's just eating food you buy from a grocery store, reading a book instead of paying for a streaming service, and canceling your gym membership to find "free" methods of exercising (e.g., running, hiking, etc.). Put money into your savings account and leave it. You will be spending it soon; it just might not be on what you originally intended.

As I write this, I am stuck between having finished my graduate degree and beginning my employment at a healthcare consultancy. The start date for my new job has been postponed for a few months due to the pandemic, which is worrisome. As a resident physician – and soon-to-be physician fellow – my wife, will not be making attending physician-level money for at least another three years. We have been successful in making ends meet so far. However, we are moving across the country to one of the largest and more expensive cities on the east coast in less than two months for our careers. Thankfully, we have been practicing fiscal discipline as best as we can, and are finding ways to make some extra money to fund our move (nothing illegal, I promise). As a result, for now, we are comfortable enough to make things work, but we would not have been comfortable if we had been a bit more cavalier in our spending habits and not made the changes we did pre-pregnancy. I am not going to lie: it has been difficult. It requires a significant lifestyle adjustment. Prior to the pandemic, I had to turn invites down from friends to go grab a drink or see a movie. You may feel obligated to do the same thing, and I would not blame you if you did. Thankfully, the alcohol bill for my wife dropped to $0 once she found out she was pregnant, so that was a quick way to cut some expenses. It does not mean that you have to stop doing these fun things altogether – just limit it. During my wife's pregnancy, she would sometimes jokingly equate the one beer or one glass of wine I would order with dinner to the number of diapers we could purchase with that instead. Thinking of it in terms like that can be stressful, but you will go through MANY diapers, so it is worth considering.

There are some larger expenses that are worth getting out of the way – assuming they are required – before your newborn arrives. For example, you do not want to endanger your new son or daughter by putting them in an unsafe vehicle. If you are like me, and like most people, you may put off car-associated expenses if you do not think they are necessary. For example, my wife really needed new tires, but her commute to the hospital is only on side streets, which have speed limits of 35 miles per hour. She rarely had to spend time on highways and mostly needed to putz around town running errands. As a result, she felt it was fine to put off purchasing new tires until later on in her pregnancy. Similarly, I put off replacing the windshield on my car as I felt it was not a necessary expense. However, we made sure both of our cars were in good shape during the third trimester as we did not want to risk putting our child in an unsafe vehicle when we could address the problem beforehand. We both had our cars serviced and had all the required maintenance completed. These were the necessary expenses, and you should think about similar things you are putting off right now, which could prove to be problematic down the road. Take care of it now. Even if something were to happen while driving your vehicle with your newborn in it and everyone was fine, it would still be such a hassle to get your car serviced. You will also have to properly take care of your newborn or find suitable childcare at a moment's notice.

It never hurts to sit down with your partner and create a budget. It does not need to be extremely detailed, but you should discuss all expenses you currently have and how you can put aside some extra money once the delivery date comes. Budgeting allows you and your lady to monitor your financial situation and project what it might look like after you implement the changes needed to adjust to the lifestyle of a parent. Ensuring that you do not overspend, particularly on your discretionary expenses, is a lesson that my wife and I learned from our budgeting process. When we sat down and talked about the things we defined as discretionary expenses over the preceding month (meals at restaurants, movies at theaters, drinks at bars, etc.), we were shocked at how much we were actually spending, and how much we could save if we made some minor adjustments. I would not consider either of us to be financial experts in the least, but the exercise of budgeting helped us better define our long-term goals and provided a roadmap by which to achieve them. There are so many expenses associated with having a baby that I failed to consider, and however minor some are (e.g., burp cloths, baby wipes, etc.), they can add up quickly. Take the time to make a budget with your partner before your new one comes so that you can define your strategy for tackling the various expenses of which you will soon be responsible for. It may be tedious, and you may think it's unnecessary, but it is worth the effort. Your free time will quickly dwindle as you begin balancing parenthood with all of your other responsibilities.

Planning your finances and setting expectations with your wife are good ways to get the ball rolling, and part of this is figuring out what your daily routine will be and how you envision things changing. Think about how you currently go about your day without a child, then factor in how things would change if you are primarily responsible for taking care of the little one. Are you going to stick with exclusive breastfeeding or rely on formula? With the former, there may not be much you can do to feed your newborn until your lady has stored up enough milk for you to do so; if the latter, then you should expect to split the feedings evenly with your partner as much as possible. I will go into more detail on feeding in Part III, but the general rule of thumb for infants is to feed them 1-to-1.5 ounces of breastmilk per hour, and we have found out that our little guy ususally likes to eat every 2-to-3 hours. Extrapolate that to a 24-hour period, and that is approximately 8-to-12 feedings every day. These figures are slightly different with formula. How are you going to split the feedings with your partner? It may simply require you to step up your game of handling chores around the house and going on supply runs.

Over the first few weeks of having our little guy home, I was doing all the chores around the house while my wife tried to breastfeed, as there wasn't much I could do to help with that until her milk had fully come in.Since she had to feed him in the middle of the night, we decided that she would let me sleep throughout the night (about five-to-six hours) and she would catch up on sleep during the day. This meant that I would have to do work around the house while taking care of our son, and it made it difficult to do much else – like going on those necessary supply runs or finding some other way to break up the day. Our situation may be a bit unique compared to others as we live states away from any family members who could help us, but thankfully we have made many good friends who helped in little ways, like delivering a meal. If you have family nearby and they are able to help you, be thankful. We definitely feel like we could have used some support, but we made it work – and so can you.

Newborns nap frequently. It is not as if you can lay them down to sleep during the day and go off and get groceries or run some other errands; you need to stay close by at all times. Our son may be fast asleep one moment, and a second later, he is awake and screaming for the boob. Plus, sudden infant death syndrome (SIDS) is nothing to brush off. Many seemingly healthy babies unexpectedly die each year because they can roll over onto their bellies and block their airways, or their face may get tangled in a blanket, and it inhibits their breathing. As a side note, do not ever put your baby in a crib or bassinet with loose blankets or other materials, as this is just a disaster waiting to happen. It is also recommended that you never co-sleep with the baby in your bed. However, if this is something that you and your lady are considering, please discuss it with a doctor in order to do it in the safest way possible. The point is that when you are home with your newborn, you are on call and need to remain responsible for their safety. This may seem obvious, but when my wife returned to work full time, and I was balancing childcare on top of Graduate School, I found it surprising on how much of my time was spent watching the baby monitor as he napped (or at least having it close by) or doing something as simple as holding and comforting him. It truly is nonstop, so be prepared for that.

Give some thought as to how you plan to travel around town with your newborn when required, such as for follow-up well-child checks. If you have only one vehicle and live in a relatively dispersed area that requires a car to get around, then the answer is pretty obvious: you need to have a car seat base in that car and ensure it is safe enough to transport a newborn. If you've got more than one car just like my wife and I, then you may choose to designate one car (presumably the one that is viewed as safer) as the vehicle in which you will travel with your child. I was nervous the first time I drove with my son in the car. The experience was kind of how I felt when I took my driving test when I was 16: hands at 10 and 2, back at 90 degrees, eyes firmly on the road ahead of me – I needed to do everything right. That is some of the most precious cargo I have ever carried, and that feeling has persisted to some degree with each subsequent trip we have taken together. Whenever we need to run errands now, there are several more steps that need to be taken into consideration. It certainly is not a bad thing, and it has made me feel like a safer driver, but it is yet another small change to my previous life that I did not give much thought to.

There are many lists you can find on the Internet or in other resources that can help identify what you will need after you bring your little one home. But you have to be pragmatic about things and do not buy something that you think you will only use once or hardly at all, particularly if space is a concern as it is for us. Of course, you will absolutely need a lot of diapers, baby wipes, and copious amounts of soap and hand sanitizer (I mean unless you like being perpetually covered in baby poop and congealed milk following spit ups). We were surprised how quickly our son grew out of the newborn and size 1 diapers, as well as how many wipes we go through daily. Be prepared to have many of these on-hand and within arm's reach. The same goes for burp cloths. When we were gathering our supplies in advance of the delivery, I joked with my wife about the ridiculous amount of burp cloths we had stored up either from our own purchases or from hand-me-downs or gifts. After three months of being a father, I am so glad we have as many as we do. We have found that distributing these in each conceivable area we find ourselves sitting with our son to be very useful as he can spit up at virtually any time. It is not that much fun to be covered in warm, partially digested milk. There are many other considerations for supplies in the first few months – especially as it relates to clothing – but I will get into that more in Part III.

You typically find out the gender of your child at the 20-week ultrasound. This is generally the earliest that the sonographer can detect whether the little one has a hang down or not, but unless you have a trained eye, there is no way you will be able to determine that yourself. My wife had an extra ultrasound around the 36-week mark just to determine whether our baby was growing as he was supposed to. We knew that we were going to have a son a few months before

that then, but during that vi...
on the ultrasound, and I still
at. All this is to say, do not b...
your child during that 20-wee...
radiologist. You can determine...
my wife and I did, through ...
testing. Essentially, this test look...
is the baby's genetic material th...
bloodstream. This can reveal infor...
whether they may have Dow...   ...e other
chromosomal condition. In other   ...ooks at the baby's
karyotype or their chromosomal make-up. This test is completely
optional, but it is worth it if you are concerned about your child
having a trisomy or monosomy condition, or if you simply want to
know the sex of your child earlier. As a side note, the 20-week
ultrasound is "the big one," meaning that this is the anatomy
ultrasound – the provider determines whether the fetus is developing
as expected, or if it has any deformities that are cause for concern.
Sometimes, a provider may find something that is *potentially* troubling,
but nothing ever comes of it. For example, during my wife's sister's
pregnancy, her 20-week ultrasound found that her son had a small
cyst-like lesion in his brain, which obviously caused her to panic.
However, some of these "abnormalities" are nothing to worry about,
and that was the case here as well – she has a perfectly healthy baby
boy who is about to celebrate his first birthday.

You and/or your lady may not want to find out about the sex of
the child at all, which is certainly not a problem. My older sister had
three children and only wanted to know the sex for her first child.
She completed her regular ultrasounds as intended for her other two
pregnancies, but asked the provider not to inform her or her
husband of the sex. They wanted it to be a surprise. Personally, I

difficult for me as I would want to know the child before seeing them for the first time, but I that not everyone feels that way. Do whatever you and y are most comfortable with.

One exercise that is very enjoyable to complete with your partner – and one that was very exciting for me to think about – is to determine baby names. Before finding out the sex of our child, we put together a list for boy and girl names. The list started at about 10 each, and we slowly narrowed it down to the top three first names that we liked the most. My wife and I have less-common names than most Americans – as do our siblings – so we wanted to choose a name that had a similar uniqueness to it, but at the same time, we didn't want a regular name that had an outrageous spelling. It was important for both of us to honor a deceased grandparent by passing down their first name to our child as his middle name. I know everyone may not share this sentiment as we all have our unique families, but we were fortunate enough to have wonderful grandparents that we wanted to honor. This was just one way that helped us narrow down, at the very least, the middle name of our incoming family member.

Determining your child's first name is difficult. I found myself thinking about how other kids may make fun of a name if it rhymes with something unpleasant (e.g., Bart and fart). Or, to make another pop culture reference, Amy Schumer initially named her son Gene Attell, but later changed it after people pointed out the uncanny resemblance that the pronunciation of his name had with "genital." I recognize that this is ridiculous, but I could not prevent the thought from entering my head. After all, the child will carry that name with them for their entire life (unless they decide to change it, I suppose), so it is a major responsibility. So far, I have named several pets I have had in my life, but that pales in comparison to the duty I felt in choosing a name for a human being. My wife and I whittled down the list of names until we had settled on three for each sex by the time of our 20-week ultrasound. When we found out we were having a boy, we slowly crossed off two and gave our son the remaining name, which we felt had a special connection to my familial history and met the criterion of being somewhat unique, at least here in America. Some couples may want to meet their little one before giving them a name, and I can completely understand that sentiment. Sometimes, you need to see if the name will fit the boy or girl before committing to it. In our case, we loved the name we chose before seeing him, and we were fortunate enough to believe that the name fits our son perfectly. Regardless of whether you want to know the sex of your child during pregnancy or you want to wait until he or she takes their first breathe, spend the time discussing potential names with your lady to ensure you are on the same page and can agree on a name that you are both proud of. But remember, she is the one carrying the baby and having to go through the traumatic experience of delivering the child – all you had to do was orgasm – so she should get the final say.

Chapter 3:
What to Expect as You Are Expecting

When my parents were discharged from the hospital after delivering my brother, who is the eldest of my siblings, my mom asked my dad, "how are we going to get through the next 24 hours?" My dad responded, "24 hours?! How are we going to get through the next 18 years?" They did just fine, I might add, as they had three more children after that and we all have turned out all right, at least in my opinion. There are countless books that cover what to expect as you are expecting a baby, but if I could distill my experience of fatherhood so far into a simple statement, expect the unexpected. As I mentioned previously, you can prepare as much as you want by reading pamphlets and other resources, but when your child is in your arms for the first time, the game changes.

You can expect a challenging time ahead, but even in the nine months leading up to parenthood, there are also some things you should prepare for. I think it is fair to say that I had a rollercoaster of emotions throughout the process, and I have shared a few reasons why so far. The baby shower, although not *essential*, is much more commonplace and is worth the experience. Lastly, your lady's body is going to change (no duh), and she is going to get quite physically uncomfortable. Get the massage oils at the ready, put a smile on, and be prepared to listen to, recognize, and respond appropriately to her complaints as you will need to become the source of comfort for her in the next nine months.

When you first find out that your lady is pregnant, you may respond with a mixture of emotions ranging from excitement to dread. I was in disbelief upon hearing the news and almost doubted if it was true until we received confirmation from our healthcare provider. I think part of this was because my wife got pregnant as soon as we started trying. I actually expected that it would take us a bit longer as it does with most couples, but I suppose we are extremely fortunate not to have this problem. Throughout the pregnancy, when people asked me how I felt, I would often respond that I was just as thrilled and terrified. I was ready to be a father, but at the same time, I was not, and I was fearful that I would not be able to do it. I was enthusiastic and anxious.

I did not know what the hell I was supposed to do to take care of a baby. My exposure to such responsibilities was limited to holding my nieces or nephews for a few minutes until they started to fuss, then I would pass them off to their parents. Luckily for me, my wife is a pediatrician and has considerable babysitting and childcare experience; so, I followed her lead. Still, I could not help but feel somewhat helpless as the delivery date drew closer. It is such a thrilling time, but scary. I do not believe that I am alone in feeling this way, as some of my friends who are first-time dads said they had the same feelings, as did some of my relatives when they were about to have their first child. This is to say that it is reasonable to expect to have this same fear, and there is no shame in admitting it. The excitement will prevail, however; as our due date drew near, I counted down the days and crossed off the hurdles (such as work responsibilities and graduate school projects) until there was nothing left to do but wait for the induction date or for labor to begin naturally.

Looking back now, I somewhat miss the anticipation of the delivery and being able to meet my son for the first time. I will go into my experience of the delivery in Part II, but I think one thing that did worry me were the many complications that could occur during delivery. This fear was partially due to my wife's exposure to many horribly sad deliveries that she had to attend as a resident physician during her rotations in labor and delivery. Some seemingly perfect pregnancies (and completely healthy fetuses) followed by an unexpected difficult delivery resulted in some babies either dying or experiencing such trauma to the point that they would never be able to live a normal life. It is important to point out that my wife was exposed to a large sample size of deliveries, so she was bound to be present for more complications as a result, and would then share those sad, and scary experiences with me. Although you should recognize that deliveries are intense – and they absolutely are – women have been giving birth for thousands of years, and medicine has been aggressively improving every year to continually improve outcomes. Be excited for this next stage of your life, and some things are worth worrying about, but do not let that fear overcome you.

We decided to have a baby shower after my mother-in-law convinced my wife to do it. My wife didn't really want to have one, because it seemed to be yet another expense that we'd have to deal with. In her words, it seemed like we were paying for another (albeit cheaper) wedding reception. I know some people who have not had a baby shower, and that is absolutely fine, too. You should not feel pressured either way, but after my experience, I am glad that we decided to go for it. We chose a rather well-known Mexican restaurant near our home to host our baby shower, because 1) it was reasonably priced, 2) we would not have to travel all that far, and we did not have enough room in our home to host it, and 3) we like Mexican food and tequila (although my wife was unable to enjoy the latter on that day). We decided to make our baby shower coed, although I know some women prefer to only invite women to it. You and your lady should decide that which will work best for you.

There are pros and cons of having the baby shower. Of course, it can be a headache to plan it all and invite everyone whom you want to attend. She invited many of her friends who lived in the same city as us at the time, and I was friends with many of their husbands, so I actually enjoyed the experience. Our baby shower occurred during the last few weeks of the NFL season, so some of the guys and I were ripping tequila shots and streaming games from our phones while the ladies played some of the common baby shower games (e.g., guess the due date, baby weight and length, etc.). It was a good time. My wife and I had made a registry, but before we filled it out, we spoke to my sisters, sisters-in-law, and mothers about what we should have on our registry. There are so many things that can be put on your registry that you will never use. If you do not know if something is worth including, I would highly recommend that you spend time with someone who has been through the process several times to refine your list to ensure you only have what you deem as the most essential. We did find that although hosting the baby shower did cost us some money (booking the room and buying the food and drink), we actually came out on top considering the value of all of the gifts that we were given. Again – it was stuff we would have had to purchase anyway, like diapers, wipes, etc., so we found it was absolutely worth the time and expense. You should not take this as me saying that you *need* to have a baby shower, nor am I saying that you *need not* have a baby shower. In my experience, it worked out well, but I recognize that may not be the case for everyone. However, I will say that unwrapping the many boxes of diapers did start to make it more real for me, as did my wife's growing belly. Our little dude was going to be arriving soon.

Watching the pregnant belly slowly grow over nine months is truly remarkable. My wife and I look back on pictures she took of herself from various stages of the pregnancy, and the difference between when she first started to show her baby bump to the last picture we took at the hospital before she was induced. It was incredible. It should come as no surprise that as the pregnancy progresses, your lady will become increasingly more uncomfortable. Her daily routine will start to be impacted in ways that you simply cannot relate. Take sleeping, for example: after many months of pregnancy, my wife could not find a comfortable position. She normally likes to sleep on her belly, but that is out of the question during pregnancy. She ordered some large pregnancy pillows to help, and they did help a bit, but it did not make a considerable difference. If this means that you have a little less room on the bed to sleep at night, suck it up. You really do not have any space to complain to someone who is growing a human inside of their body. Keep that in perspective throughout pregnancy – you simply cannot relate to what she is going through. It may be difficult for her to find a comfortable position in which to sit on the couch. Can you imagine your body changing so quickly to the point that you cannot sit comfortably? It is difficult for me to relate to that.

On a more intimate note, some women find it difficult to get in a comfortable position to do the no-pants dance. I know my wife found this positioning to be difficult, even if she still enjoyed the sex itself. She said that she felt disgusted when we tried, but obviously, I did not think so – nor would I care. For some women, pregnancy hormones can cause them to get crazily horny. That was not the experience that my wife had, but it is certainly possible. I really envy the guys whose ladies do experience that.

Your lady is going to start feeling larger every day; in my wife's words, she said she felt like a beached whale. If humor is a big part of your relationship – as it is for us – then go ahead and try to crack a joke at her expense. However, always remember that the pregnancy hormones are powerful, so tread lightly. As the pregnancy progresses, her legs and feet will begin to swell, her back will become sore, and she may get terrible heartburn. My wife's heartburn was so bad that it would wake her up in the middle of the night, and she would not be able to fall back asleep, though this may have also been due to an inability to find a comfortable sleeping position. It certainly is not a bad idea to surprise her with a nice pair of compression socks, offer to give her a back rub whenever she wants, and have a bottle of famotidine handy to proactively prevent heartburn. You should be ready to be at her beck and call because she will be going through somewhat of a miserable experience. I do not believe that I have met any woman who has said that they had "fun" being pregnant. It is a life-changing experience, for sure, but I am pretty sure every woman who is pregnant cannot wait to be done being pregnant by the end of the third trimester.

Remember to keep things in perspective and recognize that your lady is going through a lengthy and rather traumatic experience. You really should not have much to complain about, and if you do, keep it to yourself; she's going through a lot already. She is not going to feel bad for you. When my mother-in-law was giving birth to my wife, she experienced a very difficult, long labor. After some time, and while my mother-in-law was still pushing, my father-in-law mentioned that his back hurt from standing for so long. I would advise against doing this. It did not end well.

You should try to understand why your lady would not want to go to an event (e.g., a concert), a friend's house, or a bar. She is going to be more comfortable at home, and it is not like she can enjoy alcohol if you decide to have a night on the town. She is simply not going to have the same experience as you are. There may also be times that pregnancy gets her down, or it may simply frustrate her that she would not be able to do somethings as easy as sitting comfortably on the couch. Remind her of how amazing it is for a human being to be forming in her. She often says to me, "isn't it crazy that we *made* him?" Yes, it is, although she did the lion's share of the work. Sure, I played a role in the procreation process, but that role was easy. I did not have to cook him inside of me for nine months.

You need to become her source of comfort over the next nine months, and even into the fourth trimester. She is going to experience discomfort in many different ways, and you need to be there to respond and keep her spirits up. You will inevitably have some level of fear for what is to come, and that is okay – be open with your lady about that and continue to clarify your expectations of each other. But keep this in mind: before complaining about something, remember who you are talking to and what she is going through. In Part II, I will provide an overview of what to expect as you and your lady progress through the pregnancy, and it will culminate in the day of days – the delivery of your little one.

Part II:
The Pregnancy

The nine months of pregnancy are filled with anticipation, nervousness, and excitement. As the father-to-be, prepare as best as you can, but there will be surprises and curveballs thrown at you that no amount of preparation can get you ready for. I would like to provide a sort of overview of how the fetus is developing, how your lady's body is changing, some challenges my wife and I encountered, and some tips and tricks as to how we navigated these nine months. It will be a challenging experience, particularly as your lady's body changes as she continues to incubate the little one inside of her. My wife and I often joked that our unborn child was a parasite leaching nutrients off of her, making her sick, and disrupting her lifestyle. That is essentially the case, though I recognize that it is a somewhat morbid way to think about it. Lucky for men, pregnancy does not take a physical toll on our bodies; unless, of course, you find yourself putting on some sympathy weight to make your lady feel better, but I would not advise doing that.

This section will cover the nine months of pregnancy and ends with the delivery of your child or children. The first time you lay eyes on your little one(s) will almost certainly be one of the most memorable experiences of your life – I know I certainly will not forget the day that my son was born and I first laid eyes on him. Remember that throughout this period – and well beyond into the fourth trimester – you must be the source of comfort for your lady as they absolutely face a more difficult path ahead than you do.

Chapter 4:
First Trimester

The first four weeks of pregnancy can often go by without your lady even noticing that anything is different, and why would she – by week four, the fetus is no larger than a grain of rice. At this point, you may not have any reason to think that she is actually pregnant unless she is religiously peeing on a stick following a hump session that occurred around the time she ovulated. My wife did not know she was pregnant until she took her at-home pregnancy test around the six-week mark. I will say that she was taking prenatal vitamins to invigorate her body to be ready for pregnancy, but we still were surprised (albeit pleasantly) when we discovered the news. These early weeks will seem much like any other, and your lady will likely go about her business as usual.

We did unofficially schedule the times we were going to make whoopee after she began taking prenatal vitamins and pulling the goalie. Fortunately for us, it did not take us long to achieve what we set out to do. There is some uncertainty waiting before you can take a test. It is not as if a day after you and your lady had sex during her ovulation, that the at-home pregnancy test will be able to detect the pregnancy hormone called Human Chorionic Gonadotropin (hCG). This hormone typically cannot be detected by cheap home tests until about a week after her first missed period, which is when she should begin peeing on sticks for the most accurate results. There is certainly excitement over those few weeks, but even if she does have a positive test, remember that it is not uncommon for miscarriages to occur in the first trimester. If the test is positive, by all means, you should celebrate, but remain pragmatic and realistic about your situation. Set your expectations accordingly.

As everyone knows, a pregnant woman should refrain from heavily drinking alcohol. Ideally, she should not drink any alcohol throughout the pregnancy. Still, some studies have shown that minor alcohol consumption has not led to serious, deleterious consequences in the fetus. I am not advocating for a pregnant woman to get blind drunk; quite the contrary. A glass of wine here or there *may* be fine, but she should avoid alcohol as much as possible. Before the pregnancy-pee-test can accurately determine if hCG is present – and that she is pregnant – you and your lady will likely continue going about your day as usual. Many women stop consuming alcohol when they start trying, but obviously, other women get pregnant unexpectedly after drinking regularly.

My wife took her first pee test upon returning home from getting a drink with some friends at one of our favorite cocktail bars nearby. Even the days and weeks immediately before this, she had a few at home and socialized with her friends at other restaurants and bars. She felt tremendously guilty for not considering the possibility that she could be pregnant before putting a few back, and I am sure there are many other women out there who have had the same experience. There is nothing to feel guilty about – again, the fetus is barely perceptible via ultrasound even by the four-week mark. Also – just to help set her mind at ease – excessive alcohol consumption does not generally have a negative effect on the zygote (one of the early stages of fetal development) in the first two weeks following fertilization. However, some alcohol-induced congenital disabilities *can* affect the developing embryo in the third week[3], though there may be absolutely nothing to worry about if your lady continued to drink until she realized she missed her period. Speaking anecdotally, my wife definitely had a few drinks while pregnant, and our son is perfectly healthy and happy (and, just to clear the air, my wife is not an alcoholic!). Of course, when she found out that she was pregnant, she cut out alcohol altogether, as all women who are knowingly pregnant should. You may hear about women having a glass of wine here and there during the third trimester, and although many babies and children do just fine, just know that there is no proven safe amount to consume during pregnancy.

Finding out that your lady is pregnant does not necessarily mean that *you* need to cut out alcohol, but I know that those expectations can vary based on the couple. I know that my wife liked to try a sip of some wine I had here and there, and I think doing that helped her maintain some sense of normalcy throughout the pregnancy. I would definitely recommend having your house stocked with her favorite wines, beers, and/or spirits upon your return home, as you will definitely have something to celebrate!

By weeks five to eight, your lady still may not look pregnant – and she may not even realize that she is pregnant at all. My wife certainly did not know that she was pregnant; she decided to pee on the stick on a whim (her periods were highly irregular, so she was not concerned when hers did not happen). Of course, she called me upon a positive result – several positive results, in fact – and we were still in disbelief. I was perhaps even a little doubtful that it was true. This is typically the time that most couples will figure out they are pregnant, as it is reasonably safe to assume that it would not be difficult for the average woman to realize that she had missed a

---

[3]   https://embryo.asu.edu/pages/developmental-timeline-alcohol-induced-birth-defects

period. Still, I certainly would not be able to speak from personal experience what that is like.

After getting the positive result via the at-home pee test, schedule a visit with her healthcare provider as soon as possible to have them confirm the pregnancy with the qualitative and quantitative blood tests which evaluate levels of hCG in her blood as I mentioned in Part I. I was unable to attend this initial visit with her as I was on a work assignment several states away for some months. Still, I regret not being able to go. I would highly recommend to all guys reading this that you go to support your lady and hear the "official" news from the healthcare provider. My wife was kind enough to have me on FaceTime when the final word was shared with us, but I think it would have been a lot more exciting to have been there physically holding my wife's hand. This is true for all prenatal visits – be present at them as much as you feasibly can. The opportunity to have this experience is limited (I mean unless you are planning on having a litter of children), so make as many memories as you can while going through it together.

As I mentioned in Part I, if the blood tests have confirmed the pregnancy, but the heartbeat is still difficult to discern on the ultrasound, do not panic – everything may still be just fine, as it can take more time to capture the growing baby on the ultrasound at this stage. By week eight, the embryo is about the size of a pinto bean, and the eyes, ears, nose, and upper lip are just starting to take shape, and might even be visible in the ultrasound. It is typically at this point that the little one has moved from being an embryo to becoming a fetus. Your lady may still not feel pregnant, but morning sickness may begin setting in, though it was a little later for my wife.

Keep in mind that at this stage – as well as in weeks nine through twelve (i.e., until the end of the first trimester), miscarriage is still very possible, and may be even more possible if it is her first pregnancy. You may feel the desire to spread the news that both of you are expecting a new family member, but I would urge caution. I know that my wife and I wanted to tell everyone, but we hesitated until we were clearly into the second trimester. We did, however, tell our immediate family members as we felt the need to tell someone. Even if the worst does happen and she does have a miscarriage, you can always try again. My wife and I have been fortunate enough not to have gone through the experience of a miscarriage, so it is difficult – if not impossible – for me to pass on words of wisdom as it relates to that. It certainly cannot be easy for any couple, but I can only imagine that it is much more difficult for women who wanted nothing more than to carry the baby to the end to find out that they miscarried. It at least seems like it would be more difficult for women than men as they are the ones who have the responsibility of growing the child in their bodies. My wife and I have friends and family members who have had miscarriages in the first trimester, and it is a traumatic experience. Should it happen to you – and I sincerely hope that it does not – remember that it may negatively affect your lady emotionally (and certainly physically) more than it affects you.

Starting in weeks nine and ten, my wife had terrible morning sickness. She would often throw up in the mornings and sometimes even throughout the day, and her appetite fluctuated significantly. She would feel starving at one minute, then would have waves of nausea after catching a whiff of something normally innocuous. Some foods and drinks that she loved before she was pregnant just sounded and smelled awful to her now. She cut out caffeine during the first trimester of pregnancy, but before pregnancy, she loved the smell and taste of coffee. As she neared the end of the first trimester and the morning sickness ramped up, even the faintest whiff of freshly brewed coffee made her sick to her stomach and had her rushing to the nearest bathroom to purge the contents of her stomach, even if nothing was there. She also could not stand mint, which made even brushing her teeth difficult; she had to buy children's strawberry toothpaste to get the job done! She also was unable to drink regular tap water and relied heavily on sparkling water, and carbs – salty carbs, in particular – increasingly became a staple in every meal as it was one thing that always eased her sickness. In fact, she usually had a can of La Croix and a few saltine crackers on her nightstand just to combat the nausea she usually experienced upon waking in the morning.

Unfortunately, this was just the start of morning sickness for her, and it persisted for several weeks into the second trimester.. Morning sickness seems to vary quite significantly among women, with some having none at all, and others being weakened by it for much longer periods of pregnancy than my wife was. My wife also stated that some smells would be fine one day and would make her hustle to the bathroom and throw up on other days. This is to say that it is difficult to predict what it will be like for your lady, but do what you can to cut out foods and drinks that appear to be likely culprits – or at least make and consume them outside of her company. Also, do not be surprised if one evening you are cooking a meal that does not trigger nausea from your lady, but a week later, that same meal will make her puke – it was completely unpredictable for my wife. What you can do is have Unisom and vitamin B6 handy as these are frequently used to treat nausea during pregnancy, and my wife found them to be quite helpful.

As my wife neared the end of her first trimester, she noticed that she was feeling more and more exhausted throughout the day, and recognized that her pregnancy hormones were making her have mood swings. I do not recall noticing any significant mood swings personally; however, she did tell me that she could tell that the pregnancy was making her moodier some days than others. It seems like she was able to keep any unwanted or unexpected outbursts in check, which I suppose I must be grateful for. I hope you guys have ladies with similar willpower as my wife's ability to quell some urges certainly did not cause me any undue stress. Pregnancy can certainly make women feel more exhausted, and it should not come as much of a surprise. I think my wife had it a little harder than some other pregnant women given her profession, as resident physicians need to work long and odd hours, and are almost constantly on their feet, moving from patient to patient. Regardless of what your lady does, the pregnancy is going to wear her down and make her tired; let her rest when she needs it!

By the eleventh and twelfth week of pregnancy, the fetus is about the size of a plum. Your lady will have put on a few pounds as her body continues to transform for growing a little human. Remember, she is never fat at any point in her pregnancy – she is just pleasantly plump! Just kidding, do not say that. The fetus begins to actually look like a miniature person now, with fingers, and toes. Their head takes up almost half of the baby's entire body, but those proportions will adjust over the next couple of weeks. Their organs are still developing, of course – and they have a long way to go – but the first trimester is winding down. There is still some uncertainty at this stage, as miscarriage certainly is still possible. Remember that miscarriage is still possible once your lady is into her second trimester, but the probability of it drops significantly. I would still recommend waiting to widely spread the news of the pregnancy until your lady is into week 13 or possibly even week 14 for a little added confidence. Over the next several months, she is going to look more and more pregnant, and the due date will be here faster than you know it.

Chapter 5:
Second Trimester

If she has hit week 13, she is into her second trimester! You and your lady should start feeling more confident about the unlikelihood of miscarriage, although you are not completely out of the woods yet. However, my wife and I announced our pregnancy on social media halfway through week 13 (well, she did, because I never post anything on social media), as this is generally the time when sharing such news seems appropriate. Your baby's head now only makes up about one-third of the baby's body, so they are beginning to look more and more like a human being and less like an alien (which is what I thought and said ours looked like, much to the annoyance of my wife). It is wild to think that if you are having a girl – and you may not know the gender yet – the unborn girl's ovaries are already filling with thousands of eggs for when it will be her time to go through the same process. How crazy is that?

Between week 13 to week 17 is when my wife – and generally, most women – start showing that they are pregnant. Looking back at the pictures now, the baby bump she had at this stage seems so minuscule compared to the pregnant belly at term, but that should not come as a surprise. It just amazes me how much the fetus grows between now and week 40. For my wife, the morning sickness began to subside around week 15, although this is not the case for all women, and your lady may have persistent morning sickness for weeks – or possibly even months – to come. Near week 16 or week 17, my wife said that regular exercise started to become more difficult. She enjoys running outside or on the treadmill, using the elliptical, dominating the stair master, and cycling, but it progressively got harder for her to maintain the same level of workouts she sought at this point, and she had to adjust. Instead of running, she would walk similar distances in a longer period, and would slow her pace on the elliptical or stair master. Using the bike – even a stationary one – became increasingly difficult as our son continued to grow inside of her and inhibited her ability to bend in the position necessary to cycle. She adapted, and so can your lady.

I am sure that you have heard of the expression of "pregnancy glow" that some people seem to think pregnant women have, but my wife thinks that is just a nice way to call a pregnant woman sweaty. I suppose it is not far from the truth, as my wife often found herself getting overheated fairly easily. Your lady's blood volume would increase to supply the little one growing inside of her, and this can have some negative side effects. For example, your lady may experience more nosebleeds than usual, and she may start to notice that the veins in her legs have grown. It is nothing to be concerned about – it is just one of the many aesthetic casualties that accompany pregnancy. The good news is that the morning sickness may start to go away around week 16 or 17 – at least it did for my wife – but that is not the case for all women. One thing you may also notice around this time is that her breasts typically start to grow. They will continue to get a little bit larger as the pregnancy goes on, and maybe even bigger than that if she exclusively breastfeeds. My wife has been breastfeeding for a few months as I write this, and I am happy to report that she has gone up multiple cup sizes. I have found enjoyment with this change, and I am sure you will, too.

Things started to get interesting between weeks 18 to 22. My wife started to notice our son moving about and kicking hard at this point, even though it often woke her up from her sleep for the rest of her pregnancy. As I mentioned in Part I, the 20-week ultrasound is "the big one," as this is the anatomical ultrasound to determine if there are any malformations in the fetus that may cause concern; this is both from the perspective of the potential quality of life of the child should the fetus not be developing as normal, as well as if there are any concerns about the health of the mother if she does carry to term.

During my brother and his wife's first pregnancy, everything appeared to be progressing as normal until their 20-week ultrasound. After questionable results from imaging, their health care providers performed some blood tests and found that their fetus had some kind of rare syndrome that resulted in clubbed legs, clubbed hands, a cleft palate, and suspected severe mental impairment. They were open and honest with my brother and sister-in-law and told them that even if they did carry the baby to term, it was unlikely that the child could live more than a few years, but all of those years would likely be spent in the hospital. They stated that it would be difficult for the child to experience anything resembling a fulfilling life even with a presumed shortened lifespan and that the delivery would likely be very complicated – potentially even putting the health of my sister-in-law at risk. After a few days of careful thought, deliberation, and discussion, my brother and sister-in-law decided to surgically terminate the pregnancy. It remains one of the – if not *the* – hardest decisions that they have ever had to make, and they certainly did not make it lightly. I believe they made the right decision, although I know this can be a touchy subject. I sincerely hope that no one has to go through a similar experience, although I know life is not fair, and there is likely someone (or perhaps many people) faced with that same decision today. Consult with your healthcare providers, seek as many additional opinions as you like, but please, take the time to consider what life would look like for a child with severe physical and intellectual developmental disorders. My wife has cared for many young children born under similar circumstances who have barely spent a day outside of the hospital, and she has seen the toll it can take on some parents and on the child.. It's certainly a difficult way to experience life. I'm just sharing this story, and my thoughts, because it's at this stage of pregnancy that people can be blindsided with awfully sad news about the fetus. Of course, this is just one anecdotal experience, and if it does happen to you, know that you are not alone.

During the 20-week ultrasound, your healthcare provider can typically determine the gender of your child. I mentioned in Part I that there are methods of detecting the sex of the baby earlier, but it is from this ultrasound that most expecting parents usually find out – if they choose to. My wife and I had to know the sex of our child, and we asked that the provider write it down on a notecard, place it in an envelope, and we would open it together. I was returning home from my out-of-state work assignment a week after we received the concealed note, and it was very exciting to read, "it's a boy!" when we opened the envelope on our bed. We were very excited to share the news with our friends and family and decided that we would have a cake made for our dog to eat, and the inside of the cake would either be blue or pink (for a boy or girl, respectively) to reveal the gender. Some people have a bit more extravagant ways to reveal the gender, but we thought this was simple and fun, and it really fit our personalities.

The 20-week mark is the halfway point of pregnancy, and the baby can begin to hear and even respond to sounds. My wife liked to sing to her belly at night, which made me laugh. The baby is about the size of a banana at this point, and your lady can expect to gain approximately one-half to one whole pound every week until the end of the pregnancy. The baby's sex organs are developing at this stage; the boys' testes have begun to descend, and the girls' lady parts are all where they should be.

My wife says her favorite stretch of pregnancy was from weeks 23 to 27, or the last chunk of the second trimester. She felt like her belly was not so large to the point of being uncomfortable, but that it was clear she was pregnant and that the baby bump was "cute." By week 25, the baby is between the size of a ballpark hot dog and a head of broccoli. The baby's skin begins to become cloudier and less translucent. My wife has seen some babies born extremely prematurely, and their skin can be almost see-through. You don't need to worry about that.

One thing my wife and I did that was certainly not required – nor covered by insurance – was a 3-D ultrasound. I believe we had ours done around week 26 or 27. Most (if not all) hospitals do not have a 3-D ultrasound machine because it is not medically necessary for the imaging required to monitor the baby's growth over the nine months of pregnancy. There are private companies that offer the 3-D ultrasound as it affords you with an opportunity to get a clearer image of what your baby's face looks like. My wife's birthday occurred around this time, and her sister gave her a gift card to have the 3-D ultrasound performed. I do not think we would have done it otherwise, but it was a tremendously cool experience. We could clearly see his face on the screen, as well as his little body, arms, and legs. It was really interesting to see him moving around in real-time, especially when you compare this with what you are able to see on the regular ultrasound machines (which are very difficult for the untrained eye to make sense of). It was the first time we had really been able to put a face with our baby, and he went from being this sort of amorphous blob in my wife's uterus to an actual human being after the experience, at least in my mind. I am sure that there are other providers of 3-D ultrasounds in most metropolitan areas, so if you have the opportunity to do it, I would recommend it as my wife, and I thoroughly enjoyed our experience.

My wife and I had our baby shower around week 27 or 28, so we also spent some time installing our car seat base, setting up our nursery, and taking care of a few other odds and ends in preparation for the arrival of our son. As she transitions into the third trimester, the baby will progressively "cook" to completion, and it is truly an exciting time as you wait for your little family to grow.

Chapter 6:
Third Trimester

You and your lady have entered the home stretch of pregnancy – congrats! It is definitely another period of relief as you now pass into the final phase. I know my wife was very relieved at this point by not having gone into preterm labor because she really wanted to ensure that she carried our baby to term, so this was constantly on her mind. Your lady will definitely start to feel more uncomfortable, and this feeling will be exacerbated by each passing week of the pregnancy. By the 28-week mark, the fetus may be as large as a squash – nearly two pounds – so it is no wonder why she is beginning to feel more uncomfortable.

You should expect to have many more frequent visits to the OBGYN now, as it is recommended to take place approximately every two weeks until the delivery date.. Although these visits are routine for all pregnancies, I would still recommend attending each visit with your lady as your presence may comfort her – I know my wife was happy to have me attend. The visits are pretty quick, too, especially if everything is progressing as it should be. It is very exciting to see the rapid growth occurring with each passing week, and these visits with her OBGYN can set you both at ease as you have the opportunity to ask any questions or voice concerns that may come up. I was glad to have attended as many appointments, and I felt that the recurring visits helped me prepare for what was to come.

By week 32, your baby is about the size of a cantaloupe, and your lady's uterus is quickly running out of excess room. However, this will not prevent him or her from squirming around in there. As the pregnancy progressed, it was pretty wild to see my son stick his leg, arm, head, or whatever else out and misshapen my wife's belly. I would suggest searching for a few images on Google that show how distorted a woman's belly can be as the baby stretches out inside her uterus. My wife said it was very uncomfortable – and I can certainly see that – but it was the worst when our baby would bump into her rib cage. It definitely does not sound like fun, but this is just another experience that I – and men in general – will never be able to relate to… excluding Arnold Schwarzenegger's character in Junior, of course.

My wife's heartburn got progressively worse in the third trimester, which is usually the case with many women. She told me that she had a constant sour taste in her mouth as she would repeatedly experience acid reflux at all times of the day. As a matter of fact, she told me that the sour taste never really went away, but rather it got better or worse at any given time. Her heartburn got so bad that it would wake her in the middle of the night and prevented her from falling back asleep. It does not sound pleasant, and as someone who regularly experiences heartburn from spicy foods or acidic drinks, I cannot imagine it being so bad as to wake me up at night. She would joke with me that her reflux – stomach acids making their way up her esophagus and to her mouth – was somewhat of a prelude of what was to come with our baby. Our son spits up warm, chunky milk following his feedings, so I suppose the comparison was spot on. Remember to have "famotidine" in your home as your lady will likely need it to combat her heartburn, and she will definitely be grateful for you being Johnny-on-the-spot with this remedy.

Things will progress from weeks 33 to 36, much like they have before as your lady will get more and more uncomfortable as the baby continues to grow. My wife was still nervous about going into labor at this stage as it is still technically preterm, but she became more confident and at ease with each passing week. The recurring visits with her OBGYN were also helpful as she was able to set us both at ease by stating that our pregnancy was progressing as expected. Again, I would like to reiterate the importance of you attending as many of these appointments with your lady as possible, as it is comforting for her to have you present; although it may not be necessary. Serious fetal growth occurs at the beginning of week 35 as they usually put on around one-half pounds or more every week until delivery. By week 37, the baby will actually be considered full-term, but keeping the bun in the oven a little longer is still ideal. The baby is approximately the size of a honeydew melon, and with each passing day, it will continue to increase pressure on your lady's bladder, so expect her to take many more frequent trips to the bathroom.

By the last three or four weeks of pregnancy (i.e., weeks 37 to 40), your lady will be most certainly ready to be done with the experience and get the little sucker out. I know my wife was ready for it. I joked with her that our baby was essentially done "cooking," but we were leaving it in the oven until he was nice and golden brown. The baby's head will begin moving into position in your lady's pelvis, and its immune system is preparing for life outside of the womb. By week 38, the baby's brain has started to control the functions of its entire body, from heart regulation to breathing, and its reflexes are also active. Your lady is undoubtedly experiencing many backaches as she has had to accommodate the several additional pounds in her midsection over the last few months. Though, she is almost at the finish line.Braxton Hicks contractions are likely to begin to occur –

which are thought to be "fake" pre-labor pains – but may be caused by a variety of things, such as dehydration or over-exertion from exercise.. If they do get more intense and occur regularly, it is probably a good idea to reach out to your healthcare provider just to ensure all is well.

My wife was definitely ready to be done with her pregnancy once we reached week 39 as she was very confident in the health and development of our baby, though we did have an induction date scheduled a few days after her official 40-week mark. However, she would not have minded going into labor naturally, so we explored a few at-home exercises in an attempt to induce her. These included sex (I did not complain), nipple stimulation (I did not mind helping), eating spicy foods, and doing jumping jacks, among others. Although none of these interventions worked for us, I have heard of some of them working for friends and relatives, so it certainly does not hurt to explore them (especially the sex).

By now, you should have your delivery plan in place. Week 40 is considered the final week of pregnancy, but going beyond this can increase your lady's and your baby's health risk. By week 42 – if you were to get to this point – the delivery can be dangerous (not that it is not traumatic enough to begin with), so scheduling your induction date a few days after the 40-week mark is always a good idea just so you have it. Your lady could always go into labor naturally before that, and there is certainly no problem if that were to occur. My wife originally scheduled her induction two days *before* her 40-week mark, but she decided to push it to two days *after* the 40-week mark as she wanted to give her body the chance to go into labor naturally (plus, the original induction date coincided with the Super Bowl, which was unacceptable to me… just kidding…kind of). Whatever you and your lady do, be sure to work closely with your healthcare provider and have your "go-bags" at the ready in the final weeks of pregnancy.

Ahead of these final few weeks, it is obviously important to let your employers know that you are expecting a child, and you should plan for paternity leave. Hopefully, you do not work for a company that does not offer it as I could not imagine leaving my wife and baby immediately following delivery to return to work. Make sure you have a work colleague ready to handle your responsibilities as much as is allowed so you can spend time with your family and pour your entire focus into them. It will also be important to make any last-minute purchases you need and prepare your house for the arrival of your child, such as stocking up on diapers, wipes, and ensuring that all bottles and breast pumps (if applicable) are washed and ready to go. If you have a pet, ensure that you have a plan in place to have them taken care of while you are at the hospital; your fur babies are important, too. Lastly, go on any last-minute dates with your lady and do other things you will not be able to do with a baby. It will undoubtedly be a while before you can do these things again – and you will miss it – so capitalize on the freedom of not having to care for a baby while you can. I have enjoyed every day since my son was born, but I do miss the spontaneity we were allowed before he arrived.

The pregnancy is now complete. The anticipation has been building for months, and you and your lady probably can't wait to meet your little one. The time for planning is over. Get ready for one of the most memorable experiences of your life.

Chapter 7:
The Delivery

The due date – or perhaps the induction date – has now arrived. Your primary responsibility for the next several hours or days is ensuring that your lady is as comfortable as she possibly can be as she is about to go through one of the most traumatic and painful experiences of her life. As a guy, you will never be able to relate to the experience of delivery (or pregnancy in general), for which I am extremely thankful. It is intense. It can be emotional. There will be blood, and at the same time, there may be poop. I would like to begin with narrative as it relates to natural labor as compared to induction, as well as cesarean sections (or C-sections) as compared to vaginal deliveries. Regardless of what you experience, it will be a defining moment of you and your lady's life. There are many sights, sounds, and smells associated with the delivery, and I will certainly share my experience. But the first encounter with your child will leave you in awe and make you so grateful for having a lady with the strength to bring them into your life.

I mentioned earlier that my wife ultimately decided to schedule her induction date a few days after the official 40-week mark. Though she wanted to give her body the chance to go into labor naturally. She also planned to have a vaginal delivery instead of a C-section as she felt that the experience of delivering with the latter would not be the same as the "natural" way of the former. The first point I would like to make clear is that these decisions absolutely should be left to your lady to make. Sure, you can make suggestions, but she is ultimately the one that is responsible for getting the little sucker out while you just have to stand there and make her as comfortable as you can. The guy's job is so easy on the delivery day; it is not even worth comparing. Whatever decision she makes – whether it being the chosen date of the induction or C-section versus vaginal delivery – you must fully support it. However, know that C-sections often are not elective, although some hospitals and health systems will allow women to decide to pursue one if she really wants it. I recognize that some women may feel uneasy about being induced and would rather go into labor naturally, but remember that prolonging the delivery beyond week 41 can put your lady and your baby at risk. As such, I would advocate for you to convince your lady to schedule an induction date somewhere between weeks 40 and 41, should you need it. It is possible that if she desires a vaginal delivery and intends to go into labor naturally – and the official week 40 and 41 marks have come and gone – she may have no choice but to deliver via C-section because the baby will become too big. It is better to be safe than sorry, and this is a decision that should be discussed with your OBGYN as well.

Our experience in scheduling the induction date is perhaps a little unusual. I mentioned earlier that we originally scheduled it a few days before her 40-week mark but decided to switch it to two days after, just to give her body a chance to go into labor naturally. However, maternity leave for resident physicians is a joke – it is basically non-existent – so she did not want to push her delivery any further back with the knowledge that she was due for delivery and that our baby was ready to be delivered. My wife wanted to maximize the amount of time she could spend taking care of our son at home and helping me adjust to caring for an infant, for which I am extremely grateful. I had no idea what I was doing in the first few days and weeks of bringing our son home, and without her, it would have been much more difficult for me to figure it out. It would not be surprising to me if other guys that reading this feel the same way as they anticipate the birth of their first child.

One thing you should know is that being induced typically results in longer periods of labor for your lady as her body technically is not primed to go into delivery mode. The length of time for labor by induction can vary dramatically. I do not know what I would consider the "start" of labor following induction – whether it is the moment she is hooked up to an IV, when her water breaks, or when she starts pushing. My wife and I arrived at the hospital on the day of our induction around 5 A.M., and she did not start pushing until a little before midnight that same day. My wife delivered our son at approximately 12:40 A.M., so it took her a little more than 19.5 hours from the beginning of induction to the delivery. I feel like this is on the shorter end of how long labor can last following induction, as we do have friends and relatives who were induced but did not deliver until a few days later. However, the same can be said for women who go into labor naturally. I know that when my mother-in-law was giving birth to my wife, she was in labor for almost 30 hours, and mind you, she went into labor naturally. However, my sister went into labor naturally and delivered her daughter less than 10 hours later; I was actually driving her home from dinner, and her water unexpectedly broke mid-sentence, which was pretty exciting. It really is difficult to say how long you can expect the labor process to take regardless of whether your lady is induced or goes into labor naturally. Generally speaking, it seems that being induced tends to lead to longer labor.

My wife delivered our son vaginally, but I have several friends and relatives who have delivered their children via C-section; my younger sister just recently delivered twins via C-section. I will go into my experience in the following paragraphs, but if a C-section is required, it is a fairly intense procedure. It is a surgery, after all, so prepare yourself as best as you can before you head into the operating room. The surgeon will slice open your lady's midsection to access her uterus and remove the little one(s), and they must do it quickly. Your lady will be under heavy doses of pain medications, so hopefully, she only experiences minimal discomfort. It is bloody. My wife has attended many emergent C-sections during her rotations at labor and delivery, and she said the amount of blood could be quite overwhelming. The surgical/delivery team usually places a sheet vertically in the middle of the lady's chest, and the father is typically allowed to stand or crouch next to their lady's head throughout the procedure. You are free to look over the curtain if you dare. My cousin's wife had a C-section, and he told me he regretted looking as the surgeon made the incision. It made him queasy and scared for his wife. Everything turned out fine for them – as well as for everyone I know who has gotten a C-section. Just prepare yourself as it is an extreme (albeit quick) procedure.

I would like to make it clear that there are some women who intend to deliver vaginally but end up having to get a C-section. Something always has the potential to go wrong during delivery (Murphy's Law in action again). If the baby's heartbeat drops significantly while her cervix is still dilating, and the birth passage is not wide enough for the baby to be delivered, the medical staff will make the decision to conduct an emergency C-section as it is the best course of action to save the baby (and, potentially the mother in some cases). This does **not** mean that the mother failed during delivery. Some women have had the thought that they did not do something right to succeed in vaginal delivery, but sometimes it is simply not in the cards. The mother did not fail. Should your lady need to undergo an emergency C-section and that thought crosses her mind at any point during or after the delivery, squash it – she did everything she was supposed to do. At the end of the day, all that truly matters is ensuring that the little one gets safely into its parents' arms and that the mom is as safe as she can be.

You and your wife are both going to be nervous, without a doubt. She may even be a little scared, and can you blame her? She is about to have a human expelled from her body. The best you can do now is be present, be supportive, and comfort her as much as you possibly can. It is likely going to be the most traumatic (though exciting) experience of your lady's life. It may be terrifying for you – I was certainly scared throughout the entire delivery – but men have it so easy. You have been her personal valet for the last nine months of pregnancy but now is when you really need to step your game up. Get her some ice chips and a snack or two if/when she requests for it, help her use the restroom before it is showtime (as well as after), and do any other damn thing she needs to make the entire experience a little bit more manageable. While my wife and I were in the hospital waiting for her body to respond to the drugs she was given to induce labor (called Cytotec and Pitocin), I tried to lighten her mood by playing a few episodes of "It's Always Sunny in Philadelphia," on my laptop (one of our favorite shows). This did help distract her somewhat, but when the contractions started in earnest, there is really nothing that could be done to get her mind off of it. The best I could do at that point was to hold her hand, rub her back, and give her some water when she requested it.

You and your lady should give some thought as to who you would like in the delivery room (excluding the medical staff, of course). In our case, my wife only wanted me in the room. I know that in some cultures, it is more acceptable to have several immediate family members – and perhaps even extended family members – in the room to welcome the little one. That is likely to change now, considering the coronavirus pandemic, at least in the short term, so you and your lady should talk about what you two would like to do. It is an essential conversation for you two to have before showing up to the hospital to ensure any family members who are living nearby know whether they are allowed in the delivery room or not.

My wife had her water broken by the OBGYN, which helped to speed up her labor. However, after this happened, the contractions became *much* more painful for her – as well as more frequent. She had put off getting her epidural prior to her water breaking because she did not think that the contractions had been painful enough to warrant it. This was a mistake (her words). She requested an epidural shortly after that, but unfortunately for her, several other women were also in labor, and there was a limited number of anesthesiologists in the unit to administer the epidural, so she was effectively last in line to receive it. It took approximately three hours between her water breaking to when she received her epidural, and even after that, it took some time for the drugs to have an effect. Throughout those hours, my wife looked like she was in a tremendous amount of pain, and it made me worried that something was wrong. The frequency of her contractions continued to increase, and it was likely the most pain she had ever experienced up to that point. Eventually, the drugs began to have the desired impact, and the pain subsided somewhat – but it never fully went away. After the entire experience, my wife and I cannot imagine how some women give completely natural childbirths free of epidural or some other pain relief medication. There is no question that women have a higher pain tolerance than men. Do not believe otherwise. The thought of delivery without an epidural is astounding – I cannot even begin to comprehend the pain. I know that my wife would highly recommend that all women seriously consider the epidural before going headlong into natural childbirth (as would all the women in my life who have given birth), so remind your lady of that before any commitments are made. If your lady is set on natural childbirth, then more power to her.

Once the epidural began working, my wife started to relax a bit – it actually made her quite sleepy. It also made her nauseous. Over the next couple of hours – and even after the delivery – she threw up several times. Thankfully, most labor and delivery rooms are equipped with barf bags for that very reason, as this is a common side effect, so the nurse and I were able to catch the puke and prevent it from getting all over my wife. After a while, my wife's lower half was completely numb. She was unable to move her legs, feet, or toes at all, and had no sensation whatsoever. It was almost comical how "dead" her legs were. Over the next several hours and even after the delivery, she would ask me to help bend her knees and jostle her legs around to restore some blood flow and make things more comfortable.

At approximately 10 P.M., the nurse checked my wife's cervix, but she still needed to dilate a few more centimeters before she could begin pushing. The nurse recommended we turn the lights down and try to get some rest while we could. The labor and delivery unit we were in had small pull-out beds for fathers to use if needed, so I did my best to get comfortable in it. Hopefully, your hospital has better beds than ours did. I think I had a more comfortable hand-me-down futon in college. It was more important for my wife to get the rest she needed, and again, men are in no position to complain about such trivial things – particularly when your lady is about to push a human out of her. Thankfully, my wife did get some rest and slept about an hour or an hour-and-a-half before the nurse returned to our room to check her cervix once again. She was now dilated enough to begin pushing. I had managed to fall asleep before the nurse came

63

into the room, and upon hearing this news, I sprang up and began slapping myself in the face to fully wake up – I felt like I was in a trance and could not believe it was about to happen. But it was showtime.

They turned on the lights, and a nurse and one OBGYN resident came into our room to help facilitate my wife's pushing. One thing that surprised me was that they did not have her legs up like they do at a gynecologist's office. I suppose it was ignorant of me to think it would be like that, so hopefully, I am not alone with my initial assumption of how things were going to go. My wife's legs were still completely numb and immobile, so they kind of shifted her onto one side and lifted the other leg up. I was on my wife's left and was responsible for holding her left leg in a bent position – as well as feeding her sips of water between each push as the epidural (as well as the stress of the whole experience) had made her feel dehydrated. My wife, being the champ she is, did not complain or even cry out throughout the entire process.

She started pushing around 11:45 P.M. After about 30 minutes of pushing, more members of the medical staff came into the room as they knew our baby was about to arrive; so do not be surprised by the sudden arrival of more clinicians. I will be honest – going into it, I did not expect that I would want to look at my wife's vagina as our son began making his way out. I suspect some men will feel the same way. But when it started happening, it was impossible not to watch our son's little head make his way out of the birth canal. When my wife took a break for a few seconds between pushes, the nurse had her reach down and feel our baby's head. My wife reached down and missed her lady bits by about a foot – the epidural really distorted her proprioception, and it was actually kind of comical. I laughed as the nurse put my wife's hand in the correct place, which made my wife laugh, too. She kept pushing, and I could see our son's little head

64

getting closer and closer. The OBGYN resident who was delivering continued to try to widen the birth canal, which looked like it would be tremendously painful, but my wife did not seem to notice.

This is very strenuous for the lady; there is a tremendous amount of pressure being applied to her midsection to get the little one out. As such, it is entirely possible that she may poop on herself. It certainly is not unheard of – or even uncommon – for such a thing to happen. It did not happen to my wife; at least, I do not remember seeing or smelling it if it did. I was distracted by my son coming out of her vagina, and the smell of blood was very overpowering. There was a lot of blood, and she did not even bleed as much as other women do. Women often tear their vaginas while giving birth, but this can happen to vary degrees. Some women tear so badly that their vagina and anus essentially become one hole (the "vaganus"), and require the OBGYN to spend a significant amount of time sewing it back up. Fortunately for my wife, her tearing was very minimal. Recognize that it can happen, and it may take your lady a long time to recover if it does. Can you imagine your privates being ripped apart, and this is simply some collateral damage you just need to accept in order to have a child? I cannot. Also, one of the last things on your lady's mind at this point is any shame or embarrassment associated with having her privates exposed. Her tits will be out and legs spread wide for the whole room to see, and why not. It is one hell of a battle, and there should not be anything else on her mind but getting the job done.

As my wife continued to push, I found myself increasingly overcome with emotion. His little head appeared, and almost instantly, the OBGYN resident yanked the rest of him out. He was here. I looked at the clock – my wife had only pushed for about 50 minutes—what a badass. Our son was immediately placed onto my wife's chest. Fortunately for us, he did not need to be suctioned or stimulated to breathe as some babies do and took his first breaths without issue. I leaned in next to my wife and put my hand around my son and sobbed – happily. It is hard to truly express the feeling of seeing your child for the first time. It is as if nothing else in the world matters, and that their arrival has given you a new sense of purpose in life. He wrapped his little hand around my finger, and the waterworks started flowing. We asked a nurse to take a picture of us immediately following the delivery, which she happily did. My eyes are completely bloodshot from crying, but I did not care. I do not consider myself to be a very emotional person, but the experience was overwhelming. I could not have imagined what it would be like, and there is no way to fully prepare for it, but it was the single most incredible moment of my life so far.

Upon our arrival to the hospital, the nurse had asked if I wanted to cut the umbilical cord following delivery so that they could document it in our birth plan. I was apprehensive as I did not want to screw it up and destroy my son's belly button, but the medical staff made it incredibly easy. When the OBGYN handed me the scissors, she also gave me about a two-inch stretch of the umbilical cord to cut, which I did without issue. I would highly recommend other dads do the same thing as it made me feel even more of a special connection to his delivery – and there is absolutely no need to be concerned about screwing it up.

My wife's placenta was retained following delivery, meaning that it did not come out naturally as it usually does. As a result, the OBGYN had to get elbow-deep in my wife's vagina to dig it out. I tried to avoid watching that as much as possible because it looked incredibly painful. I am not sure how common a retained placenta is, but it can cause significant bleeding if it is not removed. Thankfully, after about 10 minutes, they were able to remove it successfully. I would also recommend that you look at the placenta once it is out –

it looks so cool! It is amazing that your lady is able to grow a temporary organ inside of her body to help your child develop, and now you are just tossing it away. The OBGYN gave me a quick breakdown of the various parts of the placenta because I asked – and because I had never seen one. It is just fascinating to me. However, do NOT eat the placenta, as there is no proven benefit to doing so. I am sure you have heard stories of celebrities drying it to make little pills, making a soup out of it, or even just eating it raw. My wife even heard a story at the hospital she works in of one dad taking a big bite out of the placenta right after his wife delivered it. That is so disgusting, and it has absolutely no nutritional value. My wife was also present for what is referred to as a lotus birth wherein the placenta remains attached to the newborn until it rots off (which takes between three to ten days). This is also disgusting and puts your child at risk for developing an infection, and although it could be viewed as "natural," there is no benefit in doing this. It is not recommended (and FYI, even animals sever the cord by biting through it). Cut the cord, toss the placenta (after getting a good look at it, because it is cool), and move on with enjoying the presence of your new little family member.

I will never forget holding my son for the first time. He was so small and seemed so fragile. I knew my life would never be the same, and looking down at his little face and healthy little body made me so thankful for my wife and the new stage of life's journey we were about to embark on together. Newborn skin-to-skin is recommended for both mom and dad. Of course, he went straight to my wife's breast to begin his first feed, and the little dude latched almost immediately. Skin-to-skin with your baby has been found to calm your baby, as well as yourself. It helps them cry less and releases hormone's in the baby's body to relieve stress and stabilize their temperature, breathing rate, heart rate, and blood sugar. It also helps moms to release hormones to lower their stress and promote healing. On our son's first day of life, I laid with him on my bare chest (he was wearing a diaper, as I did not want to get pooped or pissed on), and holding him in such a way as he nestled into me made me feel an even deeper connection with him.. This also made me overwhelmed with emotion again, though to a lesser degree than during delivery. He was ours, and although the thought somewhat terrified me still, I could not wait to take him home.

After months of planning and preparation, worry and excitement, your little one is finally here. The next section will cover the "fourth trimester," which includes the first few days of life, bringing your child home, and figuring out how the hell you are going to keep this child alive. You can do it. Remember, you and your lady are a team. Since this is your first child, you can tackle the responsibilities of 2-on-1. You 're going to need to move to man-on-man with your second, and zone defense with all of them after that, but for now, take some baby steps.

Part III:
The Fourth Trimester

The last nine-plus months have been leading to this experience: you are officially a dad. The medical staff will give your lady some time to recover and meet the little one in the delivery room, but you will eventually be transferred to the Maternal-Newborn Care Unit (or some variation of that) once your lady and child are stable. When my wife and I made our way over there – she was still in the hospital bed, holding our son, and I was still in some disbelief that I was now a father (and dazed from the lack of sleep).

We were admitted into our new room around 4 A.M., and both of us were exhausted (my wife was obviously more tired). The nurses in the new unit had to give us some paperwork and instructions upon our arrival, as it's the protocol, but we were too distracted and tired to understand some of the things we had to do before we were discharged a few days later, like fill out the birth certificate and social security documents. All we wanted was for the nurses to leave the room so that we could try to get a few winks of sleep, if our son allowed us. Fortunately, he never had to be taken to the NICU following delivery, so my wife and I had been able to get to know him for the better part of three hours at this point. We were able to finally fall asleep by about 5 or 6 A.M. the morning after he was delivered. Unfortunately, the beds for dads in this room were not any different than in the delivery room, but I made it work – considering the company I was in, I should not have had too much to complain about, anyway. The nurses need to check in on your baby and your lady frequently to ensure all is well. I found these pop-ins irritating at first while we were trying to get some sleep (the sleep deprivation was intense), but I was thankful that my wife and son were getting so much attention. Cherish those early moments, because once you get him home from the hospital, it is all on you and your lady to get the job done – and potentially with the support of close family members.

The first few hours and days at the hospital are muddled together for me as it was a whirlwind of an experience, and sleeping in the little pockets of time, I had distorted my perception of how long we were actually there. We had brought several DVDs and snacks to keep us entertained in our room, which I highly recommend you and your lady include in your go-bags for your hospital stay (hospital food is almost always sub-par). As time went on, we were getting increasingly excited to get our little guy out of the hospital and get him home – and we could not wait to introduce him to our dog. The first few days and weeks at home are a grind, but hospital staff will ensure you have a follow-up visit with a pediatrician usually within three days following discharge, so at least you know what comes next. Even though my wife is a pediatrician, we were still nervous about bringing our son home – now, we were responsible for keeping this little guy alive. We quickly became comfortable with feeding, cleaning poopy diapers, getting half-digested milk spit on us, making a new daily routine, and managing sleep deprivation – and you will, too. Part of this includes keeping the romance alive with your lady (presuming you are in a relationship), but it will be some time before things are *completely* back to normal. As the fourth trimester progresses, you will find your little one growing rapidly. Everyone says it goes by fast, and even in my limited fatherhood experience, it is crazy to look back and see how much he has changed in only three months. Enjoy every second of it.

Chapter 8: Going Home

My wife and I only spent one night in the hospital after the delivery. Our son was delivered shortly after midnight on a Thursday, and we took him home that Friday afternoon. As we checked off each of the requirements needed to be discharged, our excitement grew at the thought of having him home with our dog. Our son passed his various newborn screenings without issue, and he was pooping and peeing enough that we received the all-clear to leave. Before we left, a photographer came into our room and snapped some professional photos of our son. We had the option to purchase the photos after, though we understand that some people may view that as an unnecessary expense. Ultimately, my mother-in-law decided to purchase them for us and looking back now, I am so thankful that she did – and I would recommend doing the same for your child if the opportunity exists. It is shocking to look at those photos and seeing how much he has grown, and they are invaluable mementos to my wife and me.

One of the final steps of being discharged is to show a member of the hospital staff that the car seat is being installed correctly. They will follow your lady and your child outside and wait for you to pull the car around, and once they approve, you and your little family are free to go. As my wife and I drove away from the hospital (she in the backseat with our son) I found myself at high alert as I navigated home – hands at 10 and 2, back at 90 degrees, eyes firmly on the road, and going 5 miles per hour under the speed limit. It was the most precious cargo I had ever transported before, and I intended to take great care of it. Unfortunately for us, we live states away from any family members, so my wife and I were unable to introduce our son to our parents or siblings upon arriving home. However, we were still happy to have him home and start taking care of him ourselves.

Prior to going to the hospital for my wife's induction, we had stocked up on food and alcohol, so we were all set to begin parenthood without having to leave our home – even if for a couple of days. We found it useful to have nothing else to focus on except for keeping the little one alive. Those first few days and weeks are indeed survival mode for you and your lady. This little pterodactyl will screech when it is hungry, needs to be changed, or just because, and now you (and your lady) are on the hook for addressing those needs. I know that it can be a real struggle for some people to adjust to these new responsibilities; you will need to be patient and learn on the fly. As hard as it gets, remember that it gets better as they age. It is normal not to feel a super-strong bond with your child because 1) you may be super exhausted, and 2) newborns do not really reciprocate or respond to you in any way. Your child may seem like a new alarm clock that goes off at irregular, unplanned intervals that require you to do something, like feed them or change them; you cannot hit snooze.

The first few weeks are tough. I just asked my wife what she remembers about that time, and she simply responded, "it sucked." This is not to say that my wife was unhappy about being a mom and having our son home – it was just a difficult stage, and even more so for my wife. As I mentioned in Part II, my wife delivered vaginally with minor tearing, which was fortunate considering how bad things can get for some women. Regardless of how smoothly the delivery went, your lady is still going to be in pain for weeks as her body heals. Now factor in additional sleep deprivation, crazy hormone changes, and the demands of breastfeeding (if you and your lady decide to go that route). Again, men have it so much easier than women when it comes to the pregnancy, delivery, and early months of parenthood, so be sure to go the extra mile for your lady regardless of what it is. If you are planning to exclusively breastfeed – more detail which I will get into in later paragraphs – there may not be much you can do to help when your baby needs to feed in the middle of the night. This made me feel somewhat useless, since men were not designed to do such. Our nipples are completely pointless. Such a scenario requires you to find other ways you can help, like letting your lady catch up on a few hours of sleep during the day by taking care of your child on your own, including feeding him or her to afford your lady a few more moments of rest. Some women prefer their husbands or boyfriends to wake up and change the diaper before feeding, but my wife and I decided together that it did not make sense for both of us to have to be sleep deprived when she was getting up with him anyway. However, this is a discussion that you and your lady will have to have to determine what is best for your family.

In the early months of life, it's relatively easy to take care for a baby and know what to do when he/she cries out, as they usually either just need to be fed, changed, be held, or sleep (assuming that your child is continually screaming). It will not take you long to get used to newborn care, but it is a grind. The frequency of these fits can make it more exhausting, but my wife and I are fortunate to have a fairly calm baby. Regardless, the first few weeks of our son's life were challenging; they will be challenging for any parent. You will make adjustments as you and your lady identify how best to adapt to your new lifestyle; but, remember it is a test of endurance. Get through these first few weeks as it will seem like a fight for survival, which it really is – you need to keep this little creature alive, whatever it takes. But trust me, you and your lady will get through it, and then things will get so much better

My wife and I decided to get a dog together shortly after we got engaged and moved to a new state. We both love dogs and have had dogs throughout our lives, so we needed one of our own. We were fortunate to find and rescue such a sweet, goofy dog, and we quickly fell in love with him. My wife and I jokingly refer to him as our "firstborn son," even though my wife obviously was not responsible for pushing him out, like she had our human baby. Our dog had been exposed to infants and young children before and was always so interested in getting close to my nieces and nephews to give them a wet kiss. We could not wait to introduce our baby to our dog throughout the entire pregnancy and delivery – and especially while we waited to be discharged from the hospital. They were brothers, after all. Even though I know that my dog will not have a problem adjusting to his new life with a baby, I know that it is unsafe to assume that my dog would not nip, bite, or scratch my son – regardless of whether it is from a minor to a traumatic degree. My dog is very snuggly, sweet, and friendly and would never hurt anyone. However, it is important to remember that he is still an animal.

You can never assume that *nothing* will happen between your child and your dog and/or cat. I have a personal anecdote to share, but unfortunately, there are many similar stories like it with much more grim results. But it is an important reminder to keep a close watch on your pets and growing children. My nephew was about ten months old at the time, and my older sister and her husband were

74

working longer hours. My younger sister offered to help take care of our nephew when she could, which was very helpful. My older sister and her husband had gotten a loving, playful dog together before they married, much like my wife and me. Their dog is the typical Golden Retriever: goofy, friendly, and gentle. One day, my younger sister was taking care of our nephew with the dog in our older sister's living room, and she ran to the kitchen to get a glass of water. At this point, our nephew was able to crawl and pull himself up to his feet with support, but could not quite walk on his own. He was out of my sister's sight for maybe five-to-ten seconds. She heard the dog growl quickly, then ran back into the living room to my wailing nephew. Apparently, our nephew had tried to grab the toy that the dog was snuggling and sleeping with, which startled the dog who reacted unexpectedly. Our nephew was bleeding heavily from his forehead and was shrieking. I happened to be driving to our older sister's house at the time. I arrived about five minutes after this happened to see my younger sister standing on the porch panicking, talking to 911, and holding our crying nephew with a big, blood-soaked rag over my nephew's face. It was quite a sight.

Ultimately, everything turned out fine – my nephew had to get a few stitches but recovered quickly. My older sister and her husband kept their son and dog separated for a few weeks, but they slowly re-integrated each into the other's life again under close observation. Eventually, things returned to normal, and they still have the dog today. They have had two additional kids, and no similar event has occurred again. We were very fortunate to have one of the more minor pet-on-baby attacks occur in our family. During my wife's rotations in the emergency department during her pediatric residency, she saw many horrific cases of children irreparably harmed by dog attacks. Granted, some people raise their dogs to be more aggressive, but it is still in their nature no matter how well you train them or how sweet of a dog they may be to you. By all means, incorporate your pet into your child's life – we have every intention of doing it – but remember not to take your dog's good nature for granted. Things can go wrong for no reason, so just be cognizant of how your baby and pet interact – particularly once your child begins crawling and walking.

As part of the discharge process, the hospital staff will ask that you contact a pediatrician and schedule a follow-up visit for your little one within three days. There will be several visits with your pediatrician over the first few months of your wife having a baby, and all are vital to ensuring that your child is developing as expected. It also allows you and your lady to ask any questions you have. Although my wife is a pediatrician, she was still unprepared and surprised at times when it came to taking care of our son. She has begun to really appreciate being on the other side of things – actually being a mother – as she believes this experience will help her be a better pediatrician. All this means that you should not be afraid to ask your pediatrician questions about taking care of your child. The pediatrician is a resource; leverage them as much as you can.

I believe my wife and I took our son to the pediatrician twice within the first week of his life, and early on, these frequent visits are common. Do not be surprised if, during one of these visits, you see that your little one's weight has dropped below their birth weight. It is very common for this to occur, and there is nothing to be concerned about, as long as your child's weight has not dropped by more than 10%. If it drops more than that, your pediatrician will likely have many interventions to suggest to ensure that your little one fattens up properly. During the delivery, your lady is being pumped full of fluids via IV (and thus, so is your little one), so your baby's birth weight is slightly elevated as a result. I was a little concerned when I was told his weight was down several ounces from his birth weight during one of our first visits, but the pediatrician (and my wife) set me at ease by informing me of how common this is. As such, I think it is fair for you to accept that this is likely to happen to your child, especially if your lady is still waiting for her milk to come in (if breastfeeding) in earnest.

These early visits with your pediatrician will also enable you to plan out your little one's immunizations. My wife and I chose to vaccinate our son on the schedule recommended by trusted medical sources. We believe vaccinating him is both best for him as well as best for society, though I understand and recognize some people reading this may feel differently. Regardless of what you choose, please discuss this with your pediatrician as there are other options to still have your child protected from deadly diseases by distributing the vaccinations over longer periods. It is important for you to receive objective, in-person information as it relates to your child's vaccinations, so please be, at the very least, willing to discuss it with your pediatrician. Just so my position is clear: vaccines do not cause autism (and the person who claimed they do, lost his medical license); vaccines cause adults. Please consider vaccinating your child, and do your due diligence in sifting through misinformation.

It is common for many outpatient pediatric healthcare offices to have a lactation consultant available to meet with new mothers and provide some tips and tricks as it relates to breastfeeding. We scheduled several appointments with a lactation consultant immediately following visits with our pediatrician on four occasions to get some related questions answered and receive necessary guidance. If you and your lady intend to breastfeed your baby, I would highly recommend scheduling similar visits as my wife and I both benefitted from receiving that consultation. I think it is safe to say that our son also certainly benefitted, as evidenced by the accumulation of fat rolls around his body.

Chapter 9:
Daily Routine

Finding a new normal daily routine for you and your lady will take some time. As I mentioned before, the first few weeks of being home with your child are survival mode. Your primary concern is keeping this little human alive, but I think you will find out that some aspects of this new responsibility are easier than you may have expected. For example, I have a lot of nieces and nephews whom I held as infants. I was always so concerned that I might crush, drop, or otherwise harm a newborn child because I had some anxiety holding them. The last thing I wanted was for something bad to happen to them, but I found it slightly uncomfortable (and maybe even a little scary) to be holding such a fragile little creature. If you had or have similar concerns to these, they will quickly be set at ease; within the first few days of having my son, all of my apprehension went straight out the window. It became so easy to carry him in one arm while getting something else done with the other, and you will find yourself wanting to hold them more and more. There is nothing like a sleepy baby snuggling into your neck — especially if it is your child. Even though our son's grip is strengthening, and he does not mind grabbing a fistful of hair, I still love being able to pick him up and walk around the house.

Having to go about your business while holding your child is just one way your daily routine will change. You and your lady will need to take advantage of downtime – when your little one is sleeping – to get chores around the house finished, eat, use the restroom, and take care of work or other responsibilities. Of course, you can do all this when your child is awake, too, though it may be slightly more difficult. Your child is growing quickly, so they will nap and eat at regular (and usually irregular) intervals. Generally speaking, your baby's sleep patterns will change throughout the first couple of months after birth. You can expect them to sleep approximately 16 hours each day during the first month of life, and it will slowly drop to 14-to-15 hours a day by three months. The first few days after you bring your little one home from the hospital, they may sleep for longer stretches, but that will quickly change to more erratic chunks of sleep throughout the day. It was only when we had our son for about two or three months that we could lay him down for the night around 8 or 9 P.M. and expect him to wake once before 6 or 7 A.M. to feed, and even now (he is four months old), that can change on a nightly basis. My wife usually let me sleep from the evening until our son woke at 6 or 7 A.M. and I let her sleep for several hours after that. If she needed a nap throughout the day, she slept when our son would, or I would take care of him to allow her get some rest. I am not a person who can take naps, so if I had a decent stretch over the night, I could let her sleep when she needed it. That was the sleep routine we worked out, and although we both could have benefitted from more sleep – as every parent could – we both found it to be an effective way to get the sleep we needed to stay sane.

My wife and I chose to exclusively breastfeed, but it took a little bit of time for her milk to come in fully. As a result, we had to supplement with formula for the first week after bringing our son home. Our early feeding routines consisted of my wife trying to breastfeed as much as she could, and I would get a bottle of formula prepared to top our son off as we were still waiting for enough milk to come in. Fortunately for us, we only had to buy a limited amount of formula before my wife started producing a significant amount of breastmilk. My son is nearly four months old and can eat a considerable amount, but our freezers are full of breastmilk. My wife actually had to donate some of her milk to another young mom because we were running low on storage space. It is certainly a good problem for us to have, though my wife does find having engorged breasts every 3-to-4 hours both uncomfortable and annoying, especially if that pain wakes her up in the middle of the night while our little dude is still asleep.

There are innumerous benefits to breastmilk over formula, though it is important to recognize that some women can struggle pretty significantly with breastfeeding while others simply cannot do it. There is absolutely no shame in stopping breastfeeding (wholly or even partly) and relying on formula to feed your little one. At the end of the day, the most important thing is to get your baby fed so that they can work on cultivating those cute little fat rolls on their legs and arms. I will say that breastfeeding has been shown to decrease allergies and asthma (unless, of course, you and/or your lady have a strong family history). It also decreases the likelihood of obesity both in kids and later in life, decrease ear and respiratory infections, and transfer antibodies from mother to child. It also provides additional bonding between your lady and your child. I find it fascinating that my wife is keeping our son sustained through all of this early growth entirely with her body. Breastfeeding is a natural wonder, but it can be very exhausting for mom – it burns a significant number of calories every day, depending on the woman and the amount of milk she is producing.

Before my wife was able to store enough milk for me to help with feeding, she was (rather obviously) primarily responsible for feeding our son in the middle of the night. I got up with her several times in the first few weeks of having our son home to help as much as I could, but I felt pretty useless when it actually came to feeding him. There was not anything I could do to help, beyond changing him, comforting him, and handing him off to my wife to feed. If you and your lady intend to exclusively breastfeed, you will come to have a similar useless feeling when your little one wakes you in the middle of the night. Whenever my son has fussed over the last few weeks, and my wife can quickly calm him by popping her boob in his mouth, I have found myself slightly envious. She had to work several sequential night shifts when she returned to work, and thankfully she had stored enough breastmilk for me to feed our son. Regardless, when my son woke in a fit of hunger and rage in the middle of the night, it became really frustrating to have to hold and comfort him while I waited for his milk to heat to an appropriate temperature. He would rarely cease screaming directly into my face until I was able to get a bottle of warm milk in his mouth. Alas, this is a problem all fathers will need to face as our bodies are not equipped with instruments to feed them.

My wife quickly became comfortable with our son's feeding routine. If she was home, she would breastfeed him when he was hungry, and she would pump at regular intervals if she was away. I would heat between 3-to-4-ounce bottles whenever my son seemed hungry at appropriate intervals. I mentioned in Part II that the general rule of thumb for feeding infants is to give them approximately 1-to-1.5 ounces per hour. If they go three hours between feeds, then the 3-to-4-ounce bottle is likely just the right amount, though they may need a top off following a long stretch of sleep. We usually have a few bags (in 3-to-4-ounce servings) of thawed milk in the fridge for me to feed our son. If you intend to put a similar feeding system in place, there are a few things you need to keep in mind. First, do not be overly helpful and thaw a bunch of frozen breastmilk; after being thawed, milk that was frozen needs to be used within 24 hours, or else it will go bad. Freshly pumped breastmilk can be stored in the fridge for four days, but it will need to be used or frozen after that; otherwise, it will get bad. Similarly, fresh breastmilk can be at room temperature for about four hours without turning bad, but if it is left out any longer than that, it is not safe to use. You and/or your lady may forget to put freshly pumped breastmilk in the fridge or the freezer as there are plenty of distractions with a newborn, but as long as you address it within four hours, the milk is usable. Lastly, do not be flippant about spilled, spoiled, or otherwise wasted breastmilk that your lady has produced. The entire process is demanding on your lady's body, so respect the level of effort it requires of them. Be careful in ensuring that every drop of breastmilk makes it into your baby's mouth, and be quick to apologize if you happen to spill or ruin some amount.

When my wife finishes pumping, and when I finish feeding my son with a bottle, we immediately clean the devices by soaking them in soapy water, rinse them out while using a bottle brush to scrub them clean, then let it all air dry on a bottle dryer rack. We have the Boon Grass, Stem & Twig Drying Set Bundle, which we have found to be effective in meeting our needs (not to mention reasonably priced). The accumulation of these additional "dishes" that you need to wash religiously can be annoying but you have to remain diligent about keeping everything clean. Over time, you will need to expose your child to the external environment more, but keeping things clean in the early days are certainly in the best interest of your little family. There is also no need to buy expensive sterilizing equipment; unless your baby is born premature or has another underlying health issue, good soap and water will be sufficient.

This part of the daily routine was easy to adjust to, and a closely related aspect was his other biological functions. What goes in must always come out. It is pretty hilarious to hear a little baby blast a nasty, wet fart. There will be many of such episodes of flatulence, though that should not come as a surprise. Whenever our son is eating, we are always expecting him to let one fly, and he usually does not disappoint. He poops an extraordinary amount – it never seems to cease – but he is happy and growing ahead of schedule, so we cannot complain. Your little one will need to be changed regularly. Sometimes, your little one will have blowouts where their expulsion of the poop from their bodies would be so powerful that it went up to their backs or down their legs, beyond the confines of the diaper. These are not particularly fun to clean, but it always seems that our son is in such a happy mood when we are cleaning him up following a blowout, so you may get some happy baby babble and smiles as you do it. I think it is safe to say that we change our son's diaper approximately 10 to 12 times each day, but that can vary. We have a nice changing station with fresh diapers, baby wipes, a wipe warmer, Desitin, hand sanitizer, and a place to lay him down. We open the dirty diaper, cover his penis with a wipe so he cannot hose us down (he still has, on several occasions), wipe him clean, move him onto the new diaper, spread Desitin between his little butt cheeks to proactively prevent diaper rash, cinch the diaper, throw the dirty diaper away, clean our hands, dress the little dude, and good to go. Repeat. Repeat again, and again. You will reach a point where you find yourself going into autopilot and getting this done. I had changed a minimal number of diapers before having our son, and I adjusted very quickly to the new routine. You will too.

Your little one will not only poop and pee an ungodly amount but also spit up warm, congealed milk. This can and will happen at virtually any time, even if it has been a few hours since the last time they ate. My wife and I have burp cloths distributed throughout our house because we never know when our little dude is going to blow chunks – we simply know that it will happen. If he is not spitting up, then he is producing an unnecessary amount of drool. Either way, he will eventually soak himself – and you – and require a wardrobe change. Sometimes, our son can go for 24 hours in the same outfit. He may have some spit up here and there, but for the most part, he is pretty clean. Other days, he may go through five or six outfits. Just today, the day I write this sentence, I put him in a clean onesie and fed him only for him to have a blowout up his back and spit up down his front within an hour. Expect that this will happen, and have new clothes at the ready for when it does. Also, do not be surprised if some of their spit-ups are of the projectile variety. I was recently holding my son facing me. We were having some fun, and I was making him giggle, then out of nowhere, he barfs half-digested milk all over my chest. I look down at the mess and am disgusted, but then look at my son's huge smile and cannot help but laugh myself. Good times. Be ready for the pooping and spewing disasters, and know that you will quickly acclimate. I am told that things get much worse once you introduce solid foods, so I have that to look forward to in the next few months.

We bathe our son, on average, about once each week. Of course, if he is extra disgusting and needs the "cheese" cleaned out of his various folds, then we will bathe him more frequently. Luckily, babies do not yet have body odor, and frequent bathing can dry out their skin (and we live in a dry climate). Although it typically is not a daily occurrence, my wife and I have found that we both need to be present to effectively and completely bathe him. We have a little baby bath which we fill up with soap and warm water. I hold his head and neck in place as I clean his scalp, arms, and neck, while my wife cleans the rest of him. The first few times we did it, it felt like a drawn-out process that took a little while to get used to. However, now we have the routine down and can get him in and out within a few minutes. You will also quickly adjust to the process. I would recommend keeping the 2-on-1 approach to bathing your child – at least in the early months – as it is safer. I would also say that our son seems to love his baths, so my wife and I have some fun with it.

I would be remiss if I forgot to mention something about the shaken baby syndrome in a blog for first-time dads. It is absolutely normal for you to feel frustrated when caring for an infant. I know that I have been frustrated on several occasions, with some of those times being worse than others – especially when I could not figure out how to calm my son down. Shaking a baby is inexcusable; it can cause severe brain damage or even death. It seems like such obvious advice to an outsider, but only until you have the responsibility to take care of the restless, pissed-off baby will you understand how some parents cave in to that impulse. If you ever find yourself getting more and more frustrated and you cannot seem to calm your baby down, lay them carefully on their backs in their crib, bassinet, or some other safe place and walk away. Step outside, call someone, go into another room and flip on the television, or find some other way to excise yourself from the situation until you are able to think clearly again. Take deep breaths. It can get very frustrating – I think it is safe to say that every new parent can *expect* to get frustrated in some way – but there is no returning from shaking a baby. Lay them down and walk away.

It is important for your family to stay active, including you, your lady, and your baby. The sleep deprivation associated with having a child is real. My wife and I have had several days where we wanted nothing more than just to nap on the couch when our son allowed us, and we found it difficult to get the motivation to exercise. Fortunately, one of our friends bought us a jogger that is compatible with our car seat, which allowed me to go on a run with my son securely strapped in. I found out that remaining active by running really helped me to cope with some of the stress and nerves of my new responsibilities, and it also made me happy that I was able to give my wife a break. My son loves being pushed in the jogger; it seems to rock him to sleep almost every time. It also provides me with a minimal upper-body workout – at least, more so than running without the jogger – so I have found it to be somewhat of a full-body workout. My wife has also been able to keep active by doing at-home workouts and using our stationary bike. For some women, it can be difficult to return to running as their bodies are still recovering. My wife is still recovering and is only able to run short distances before some pain in her pelvis sets in, but one of her friends who also recently delivered has had no problem returning to running. It can vary significantly, but we have both found exercise to be a crucial part of our daily routines – even if it is as simple as walking with our son in the stroller.

My wife and I have daily workout routines that we try to maintain ourselves, but we also have a little routine for our son as well. You have likely heard of "tummy time" for infants, wherein you lay them on their stomachs while they are awake. These exercises are crucial for your baby's motor, sensory, and visual development. It helps to develop the core muscles of their shoulders, neck, and back, allowing them to quickly do such things as hold their head up unsupported. It is also a helpful way to possibly prevent positional plagiocephaly, otherwise known as a flat head that some babies may get from laying in their bassinet or crib. We try to get our son as much tummy time each day as it is recommended that they achieve at least an hour every day. We usually break this up into various installments as our son will typically begin fussing after several minutes and need to be picked up. Once your baby begins crawling (usually between 6-to-9 months), the development benefits of tummy time usually come to fruition, so it is not typically necessary to continue after that point. However, it is still a good idea to have them in the prone position (i.e., on their stomachs) during playtime to help their muscles continue to develop. At any rate, exercise for all family members is essential to stay healthy and sane (for you and your wife's sake), and is critical for the development of your little one.

It may be difficult to adjust to your new daily routine of being a parent to an infant. It did take me a little time, but now I cannot imagine life without my son. You and your lady will figure out how to best make things work so that your new routines are manageable, but remember to remain active and stay calm when faced with the frustrations that accompany this drastic change in your lifestyle. Although our lives have changed in immeasurable ways, we have been able to adjust without considerable effort. You can, too.

Chapter 10:
Keep the Romance Alive with Mom

Although your priorities may have changed with the birth of your child, it is critical that you and your lady keep the romance alive throughout this tumultuous time (of course, this is all assuming that you and the mother of your child are a couple). You and your lady have just been through a life-altering event together, but care for an infant does not require you to sacrifice your intimacy with each other; however, the extent of that intimacy will need to be limited, at least temporarily. Your lady's body needs time to recover, so it will be a while until things completely return to normal. In the interim, show her your affection and appreciation in other ways and be willing to go the extra mile for her regardless of what she needs.

Generally speaking, assuming the delivery went smoothly and as expected, it is recommended that women refrain from having sex – or from having anything in their vagina – for at least six weeks following the birth of the little one. It could be longer depending on the severity of vaginal tearing, but this is typically the minimum amount of time. This recommended timeframe is true for both vaginal deliveries and C-sections. As part of the hospital discharge process following delivery, your lady will need to schedule a six-week postpartum check-up to ensure that bleeding has stopped, and in the case of a C-section, to ensure the incision is healing well. It is usually during this visit that the healthcare provider will determine if your lady's body has recovered enough to engage in the sexy stuff with you again. But even if the all-clear is been given, recognize that it can take even more time for some women to *want* to engage in it. After all, your lady did just push a baby out of her or had it otherwise removed from her body, so she very well could still be in pain (not to mention sleep deprived) and need more time until they feel back to their normal selves.

One very stressful time that guys never have to experience and cannot relate to is the potential fear or anxiety your lady may have as it relates to her first bowel movement after delivery. Just so there is no confusion, I mean the first intended bowel movement after delivery, as some women may poo a little during delivery itself (lots of pressure and pushing localized in one area – what do you expect?). Depending on the severity of vaginal tearing, some women could be outright terrified at this time. The space between the vagina and anus is really not that far, so there is reason to be afraid that any tearing that occurred during delivery could occur again. This is especially true for women who need to receive an episiotomy during delivery. The contents of these canals are not intended to mix, so the experience most people take for granted a few times each day could be truly terrifying to a new mother.

It is recommended that new moms try using laxatives, such as MiraLAX or Colace (or some other variant to obtain the same result), to ease the process as it is very common for women to be constipated for several days following delivery. This could be due to several casual factors such as long labor with little food, pain relievers (i.e., an epidural) during delivery, or that the woman is just too scared to try. It is also very typical for women with C-sections to expect to spend three to four days before their digestive system starts returning to normal. Surgeons were just digging around in her midsection, after all, so I guess that should not come as much of a surprise. Regardless of the reason, ensure that your lady has these necessary laxatives to simplify things as much as you can. She also deserves to eat and drink whatever she wants in order to dominate the delivery, so you are actually responsible for ensuring that whatever she wants passes through her body seamlessly. There may not be much that you can do actually to assist her when game time arrives, but recognize that this can be a scary experience for her. So, you will have to support her as much as you can (i.e., do not be hesitant or dismissive when talking about her pooping).

Your lady will have residual bleeding for several weeks following the delivery, assuming she delivered vaginally. During the first few days and weeks, she will need to wear a sort of diaper to help address the bleeding and any other bodily functions she temporarily loses control of. These diapers – at least, the ones my wife had to use – were also large enough to fit some specialized ice packs to help with the swelling of her lady bits. As your lady recovers and her bleeding lessens, she will move from those diapers to pads. The six-week recovery period I mentioned earlier is the general guideline where you would likely see no continuous bleeding. Still, some women may continue to have bleeding or spotting for weeks after that. My wife had residual bleeding up until seven or eight weeks following the delivery. Just recognize that this bleeding can persist for a while, so it should be easy to forgive her if she is not in the mood to get the physical romance started up right away. Even after she does, it is possible that more bleeding can occur.

My wife wanted to exclusively breastfeed, and her body had no problem delivering. One thing that I had never given much thought to is the sorts of blisters (called milk blebs) that form on some women's nipples with continued breastfeeding. Apparently, this does not happen to every woman, but some women (my wife included) have ducts that get clogged with milk due to improper latching, shallow sucking, or feeding at unusual angles. She describes the pain as milk being backed up in her breast with something impeding it. I think the closest comparison I can make for guys is the piss following ejaculation. Some residual semen may be backing up the hose, but once the urine breaks through, it is a very satisfying feeling. For my wife to relieve some pressure she has experienced, she has, at times, dug out a milk bleb with a safety pin. This is **not** recommended; she is just metal as f***. It worked, however, and she said the relief was instantaneous. It was also followed by a long, strong stream of breastmilk out of that spot for around 10 seconds. My wife continues to get milk blebs but has gotten better about managing them to some degree. Recognize that this can occur, and feel free to seek some more conventional ways of dealing with it. If milk is not drained properly, it can result in mastitis, which is an inflammation of the breast tissue. This can be both painful for your lady as well as cause flu-like symptoms. My wife had mastitis and was required to take an antibiotic to treat it, but all turned out well in the end. Her boobs felt like rocks when it was at its worst, so I cannot imagine the pressure she must have felt. Even after the delivery, the little one can and will wreak havoc on your lady's body.

There are some additional leftover side effects of the pregnancy and subsequent delivery. For example, some women experience postpartum hair loss. My wife claims that her hair has been coming out in clumps. I can back this up as she leaves her hair clinging to the shower wall if they are not clogging our drains. My son is nearly four months old, and my wife has only recently started noticing she is losing some hair. Not all women experience this, but it is not uncommon. Fortunately, things start improving around six months after delivery, but that can vary depending on the woman. Additionally, some women form a fairly prominent linea nigra, which literally translates to a black line, forming from below to above her belly button; it is like her body's Prime Meridian. Some women have a very distinct line, some have faint, while others do not have them at all. It may be present on women for the remainder of their lives to varying degrees, while it can disappear altogether on other women. The skin in this area is stretched a tremendous amount over the nine months of pregnancy, so it can also leave prominent stretch marks or distort the belly button. My wife had a pierced belly button when she was a teenager, so her belly button is all kinds of disfigured. She was lucky not to have gotten significant stretch marks, while other women can have them all over their bellies. I do not really care, though — and you likely will not either. These are just some other lasting side effects of becoming a mother. I am sure it makes you thankful to be a guy, so you do not have to go through all of this — I know that is the way I feel. But it is remarkable what the female body is capable of.

After the first or second time (maybe both) that we started having sex again, she had some additional bleeding, so we waited a while before we did it again. Like I mentioned previously, she did have some minor tearing but was fortunate when considering what some women need to deal with. It was painful for my wife to begin having sex as she said it felt like she had some scar tissues that were still healing. This pain persisted but lessened over time, but even now — four months after the delivery — there can be some pain for her during sex. I assume this is likely true for at least half of other new mothers out there. All of this is to say that I am still experiencing the journey back to normal with my wife, so any words of wisdom I can impart are limited. Give it time, and shower her affection in other

93

ways. Furthermore, do not forget contraception, unless you intend on having Irish twins.

It is never a bad idea to buy your lady chocolates, candy, flowers, or anything else she loves. Even a small gesture of your appreciation is helpful, as is continuing to do things to make her life easier. My wife said that one of the most helpful things I did for her throughout these early weeks of parenthood was ensuring that she always had a drink or a coffee next to her when she is breastfeeding. I also cook a bit more and let my wife nap while I take care of our son when time allows. She says that these rather minor things actually go a long way, so think of similar methods of simplifying your lady's life as she recovers from the delivery. It has helped my wife and me adjust to the new lifestyle together, even though there are some other continued challenges she needs to face on her own. You can be romantic and intimate, and show your appreciation in many ways. But you never can return to normal, because now you have a little one to take care of together. You showing the initiative to get up in the middle of the night to change a stinky diaper may just be the sexiest thing you can do for her right now. Listen and respond to her needs, and never forget that she went through hell to get that little one in your arms.

Chapter 11:
Change Happens Fast

After looking at pictures of our son from merely three months ago, it is astounding how much he is grown and changed. When you first bring your child home, they are like a little alien creature that screeches when they are hungry, makes small glances across their little fields of vision, and do not respond much – if at all – to human interaction. I know that it can be frustrating to want to engage with your child right away, but the truth is, they cannot really do much at all. However, things will quickly change. It was not until our son reached two to three months old that he began to have noticeable reactions to me. I can now make him smile and giggle, and we have little baby-babble conversations as he has begun finding his voice. I look forward to seeing his progression, but you do not really notice the changes when you think of it day-to-day. As with anything, it will take a little time for you to notice his changes in size and cognitive development, but it will be crucial for you to capture as many moments at each stage along the way.

My wife and I had stored up a considerable amount of hand-me-down clothing and other baby supplies. We were, after all, the last of either of our siblings to have our first child, so I suppose that worked to our benefit. We were given various clothing sizes for our son, from infant, three months, three-to-six months, and even up to a year. I thought it was kind of ridiculous how many clothes we were gathering, but my wife assured me that we would work our way through all of it. She is right, so far, and I have no reason to doubt it on our next child. Our son quickly outgrew his infant clothing and was outgrowing his three-month clothing around the two-month mark. It is insane how quickly he grew. Granted, he is a bit chubby, but he is also growing considerably in length. We are now putting the clothes he outgrew in storage until our next child, because why would we bother buying new stuff that will be outgrown just as fast? We were only able to get our son into some outfits once before he outgrew them, which was both exciting and disappointing. Particularly when we bought a shirt that matched one of ours, such as The Office's "Regional Manager" (dad) and the "Assistant to the Regional Manager" (baby). Fortunately, my wife did get one photo of us matching in these shirts.

Baby clothes can be found for low or reasonable prices, but I guarantee that you could find some free hand-me-downs if you just spent a little bit of time searching on the Internet or talking to family and friends. My wife and I have hardly purchased any clothes for our son thus far, and are glad we reached out to some friends and family to get their old baby clothes. Many baby outfits are unisex if that sort of thing matters to you, but you really should not care. Putting a baby girl in blue or a baby boy in pink makes no difference – they are not going to care and will likely just poop and spit on it all the same. Parenthood is known to be expensive, so look for ways to save money like this. There is absolutely no shame in using hand-me-down baby clothing. I am also sure that other parents who are done having babies will be very happy to have you take at least some of their baby clothing off of their hands. I would highly recommend that you look for ways to save on some clothing expenses, particularly in the earlier stages of development, as your little one will have some rapid growth. Take some time to remember to appreciate this as each day passes, because it will be quick.

This time is temporary. Sure, it might get frustrating at times when you and your lady are tired, and you just cannot figure out what your little one wants, but 20 years from now, you may look back on this time more fondly than you think you will. I was the third of four children, and when my parents had me, they were both younger than I am now. I had bad childhood asthma, which I have since outgrown, but it was particularly worrisome when I was an infant. My dad would often hold me on the porch outside of our house in the middle of the night when I was having trouble breathing with the hope that the cool air would help. He says that at the time, he was both worried about me and maybe a little frustrated, as he was also tired from taking care of an infant and two young children while working long hours. However, he told me that he thinks back on those nights fondly because it was a bonding experience that only he and I shared. I try to keep that in mind when I am up in the middle of the night feeding my son or taking care of him in some other way.

There may be some annoying aspects, sure – but the experience is all-inclusive and fleeting. Remember that every stage of your little one's development is temporary. You may not know what they want when they seem to fuss for no apparent reason. How would you act if you could not use words to express your emotions? Things get better yet more difficult as your little one grows. First, it is difficult to understand what they want (a problem which could persist for years – toddlers are regularly guilty of temper tantrums), but when that gets easier, they will begin to become mobile as they start crawling and walking. Take some time to appreciate how your little one changes over the next few days and weeks, and remember that the entire experience is temporary. You always hear stories of parents saying that they cannot believe that their child is graduating from high school or college, or is getting married – to the parent, it was just yesterday that their child was a helpless baby. It makes you think about how you want to make the most out of the experiences you will share with your little one; at least, it does for me.

One piece of advice that my wife's sister gave us was to record videos of our son with our phones – in addition to taking countless photos, of course. We have taken that to heart and routinely watch videos of him earlier in life and compare him to today, and the changes are incredible. This just reiterates the point that each new day of life with your little one will be a little bit different than the one before it. There are so many little moments that occur throughout any given day that are worth recording and remembering forever. Even if it is as simple as your little one wrapping their tiny hand around one of your fingers, them cooing up while they stare at you, or maybe it is just a memorable blowout disaster of Chernobyl proportions. Record these moments as much as you can, because you do not know just how fondly you will look back on this time in 20 years, and it will be helpful and heartwarming to have this evidence.

Conclusion

Becoming a father is such a rollercoaster of an experience. No amount of written material can help you fully prepare, and my wife and I continue to be surprised as we navigate our way through it. After the initial efforts of planning for and attempting to conceive, to the nine months of pregnancy, and through the arduous delivery, you and your lady have had some time to get your heads around this. For me, the entire experience has been everything I hoped it would be so far. I am excited to see my son every day and see him continue to learn and develop. At some point, you will inevitably want a break and have a day away from your child. However, I guarantee that within a few hours of being separated from your little one, all you will want to do is hold them again. They become part of who you are, and your outlook on life may begin to change if it has not already. Everything you do now involves your little one.

The goal of any generation is to make life easier for the generation that comes after it. I will keep that in mind as my son continues to grow, as well as for any additional children I have. It is my duty to ensure that they are better off than I was. It is all of our duties as parents. I hope readers have found this information helpful as they navigate their way through this tumultuous time. It is exciting, it is scary, but it has been worth it. I know that things will become more difficult for us as our child begins to walk, gets through the "terrible twos," and even through adolescence, but I know that my wife and I can handle these challenges together.

Remember that you and your lady are a team. You are now parents. Time will not stop, so enjoy the little things and be sure to capture as many moments as you can. Good luck!